Rolleround Oz

RolleroundOz

Reflections on a journey around Australia

SIR ROGER CARRICK
BRITISH HIGH COMMISSIONER
TO AUSTRALIA 1994–97

ALLEN & UNWIN

Maps and calligraphy by Roger Carrick

First published in 1998 by
Allen & Unwin
9 Atchison Street
St Leonards NSW 1590
Australia
Phone: (61 2) 8425 0100
Fax: (61 2) 9906 2218
E-mail: frontdesk@allen-unwin.com.au

National Library of Australia
Cataloguing-in-Publication entry:

Carrick, Roger, Sir.
RolleroundOz: reflections on a journey around Australia.

Includes index.
ISBN 1 86448 952 9.

1. Carrick, Roger, Sir—Journeys—Australia. 2. Carrick, Roger, Sir—Diaries. 3. Ambassadors—Great Britain. 4. Ambassadors—Travel—Australia. 5. Australia—Description and travel—1990– . I. Title.

919.40466

Set in 12/16 pt Simoncini Garamond by Bookhouse Digital, Sydney
Printed and bound in Australia by Griffin Press Pty Ltd

10 9 8 7 6 5 4 3 2 1

For Hilary, without whom...

for John, Leandra, James and Emma,
who could not visit us while we were
living in Australia

and for Charles and Belinda,
who did.

The publisher and author wish to express
most grateful thanks to Rolls-Royce Motor Cars Limited
for their interest and support

FOREWORD

1997 was a landmark year in boosting Australia's long and friendly bilateral relationship with Great Britain. Sir Roger and Lady Carrick played an invaluable role in presenting a new image of Great Britain to Australia, not only within the Canberra community, but across the length and breadth of the enormous Australian land mass.

I know that among many it was considered out of the ordinary to take the High Commissioner's Rolls-Royce on tour around Australia. It turned out to be a hugely successful activity. Sir Roger was just the sort of person to initiate new approaches to Great Britain's representation in Australia. RolleroundOz was a fascinating trip which has been skilfully chronicled by Sir Roger. I was sorry that it was not possible for him to take my advice and travel by rail for some of the trip—from Normanton to Croydon in central Queensland!

As Deputy Prime Minister, I enjoy getting to know Ambassadors and High Commissioners from across the world. Most are posted to Canberra for a couple of years and then replaced. Sir Roger and Lady Carrick will always be remembered by so many in the Australian Parliament and the wider community. Their representation of Great Britain was superb and the big 'rolleroundOz' is testimony to their energy, professionalism and spirit of fun.

RolleroundOz breaks new ground in giving an excellent account of broadening out diplomatic endeavour well beyond Australia's capital of Canberra. It was only a diplomatic promotional coup to Roller around Australia, but also a bonus to have compiled such a comprehensive diary which in turn, will help to promote the great outback of Australia.

The Hon. Tim Fischer MP
Deputy Prime Minister of Australia, Minister for Trade

CONTENTS

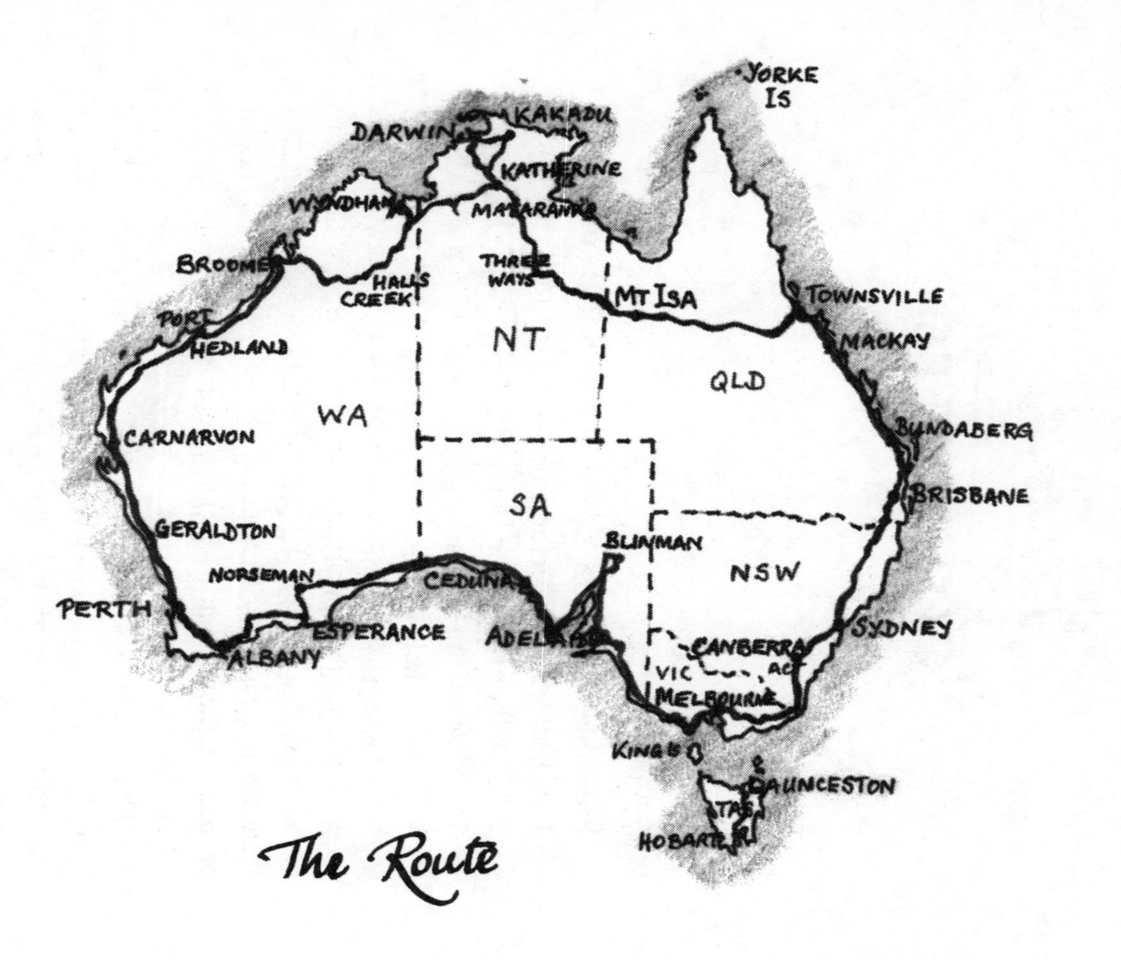
YORKE IS
DARWIN
KAKADU
KATHERINE
WYNDHAM
BROOME
HALLS CREEK
THREE WAYS
MT ISA
TOWNSVILLE
PORT HEDLAND
NT
MACKAY
QLD
WA
CARNARVON
BUNDABERG
SA
BRISBANE
GERALDTON
BLINMAN
NORSEMAN
CEDUNA
NSW
PERTH
ESPERANCE
ADELAIDE
SYDNEY
CANBERRA
ALBANY
VIC
MELBOURNE
KING
LAUNCESTON
TAS
HOBART

The Route

Preamble: Why do it?

Why indeed?

One of the duties of a High Commissioner or Ambassador towards the end of a posting in this huge continent of a country is to visit each of the Australian States and Territories to pay farewell calls on governors, premiers, lord mayors, opposition leaders—and other leaders of political and economic life. This is not a matter, as some might believe, of quaffing farewell cocktails. While there certainly is an element of thoughtful hospitality, serious business is done in the pursuit both of joint interests, and of each country's and each economy's interests in the other. As Hilary and I contemplated these farewell calls, it seemed a short time indeed since we had flown to each State and Territory within the first three months of our tour to make our introductory calls, and thereby to learn a great deal that was to make the remainder of our three and a quarter years in Australia so interesting and productive, and such fun.

But why, Hilary asked, should we do it the same way again, by air? We had many times visited the State capitals and main centres—I more often than Hilary. We had flown in light aircraft over some of Western Australia and much of far north Queensland. But we had mostly missed out on life between the airports. We had driven in the official Rolls-Royce a couple of times to Melbourne, once to Adelaide and countless times, of course, to Sydney, only three and a half hours away. Why not, Hilary suggested, drive all around the periphery of Australia in the Rolls-Royce, add something unique and worthwhile to the year of *new*IMAGES, and try to do some extra good for UK Ltd?

*new*IMAGES was a year-long, Australia-wide campaign to update and correct the inaccurate, outdated and excessively lingering perceptions in the minds of Australians of Great Britain and the Poms; and to create catalysts for future, mutually advantageous partnerships. There was good evidence, including from informal surveys, that modern Brits and modern Aussies were reading each other wrongly, to the detriment of both. There was also a good argument that while the trade and investment relationship between the two countries was remarkably strong, it could be stronger yet, to mutual benefit.

*new*IMAGES was the largest promotion of its kind ever undertaken by the British Government. It involved United Kingdom and Australian businesses in much sponsorship—and commensurate benefits. It covered British people and British endeavours in fields from science and technology through a broad range of cultural and academic efforts to hard-nosed commercial and political themes and undertakings. There were over 180 events throughout Australia. A lot of hard work and resources were involved. We wanted to see for ourselves the impact of all this effort by the Foreign and Commonwealth Office, the British Council, the Department of Trade and Industry, the High Commission and Consular offices, and many counterpart organisations and companies in both countries.

*new*IMAGES had been approved by the then Prime Ministers Paul Keating and John Major, and was subsequently endorsed by both their successors, John Howard and Tony Blair. John Howard participated personally and enthusiastically in the national launch of *new*IMAGES in Australia, and his government organised a parallel effort, also called *new*IMAGES and with the same objectives, in the UK.

To drive around the country, surely, would also provide time for careful reflection before drawing conclusions from three and a half years as British High Commissioner in Australia (or as one young cricketer I bowled in the annual cricket match we played against the Lords Taverners called me, the Head Pom). Another duty for retiring Heads of Missions is to write a valedictory despatch to the Secretary of State in London. I could draft that when it wasn't my turn to drive.

There were risks. It would be easy enough for our efforts to result in negative press in both Australia and the UK. The old image might prevail, of a senior official parading around the country on a stately progress, showing the flag but doing little or no real work. But with care and forward planning, with a good press release, with effective work by staff in the High Commission and our

Consular posts around Australia, and with luck, we might catch the Australians' imagination. We also believed there was work to be done and fun to be had; that we would enjoy dramatic and varied scenery, flora, fauna and climate all around this vast continent; and, perhaps above all, that we would meet Australians who cared little for things international or even much about Australian Federal or State governments: real people in the outback and around the coasts—from jackaroos to Aboriginal leaders. We knew there were plenty of Australians who cared little for Canberra. This is a familiar phenomenon in countries with political capitals—many Californians try to ignore Washington, for example. We thought Canberra the best by far of the 'artificial' political capitals around the world, and greatly enjoyed living there: we thought we might seek converts to our view.

We counted the costs. Our estimates showed that to go by Rolls-Royce would probably be cheaper than flying. And so it turned out, by a considerable margin, on which the office accountant in Canberra congratulated us.

We spoke to Rolls-Royce, who were distinctly keen. We talked with Stephen Timperley, Managing Director of Fox, Rolls-Royce & Bentley in Sydney, and planned a little occasional light service and a few checks—all that would be required in 17 400 km of driving around Australia.

I was to learn later, and to my surprise, that purist devotees of the marque believed that one should never abbreviate Rolls-Royce to 'Rolls'. The purist view, apparently, was that there should be no abbreviation at all, but that if there really had to be one, it should be 'Royce'. But then, that was the purist view. We would stick to

'Rolls' and would not eschew 'Roller'. A young Aussie lady taking a year off her accountancy studies to pump petrol and toast sandwiches in an isolated roadhouse in the north of Western Australia was, however, to provide the definitive statement: after careful appraisal of the car and much consideration, and with equal seriousness, she told me, 'Mr Royce did a fine job'.

Hilary and chauffeur Murray Versluis did the route planning and a great deal of research. The result was a 33 days' exercise, 25 of which would involve, at least in part, driving the route; and the remainder would be devoted solely to calls and other business. The three of us would share the driving: two hours on, four hours off, in principle; although Murray would start most mornings. We would carry no extra petrol, nor any camping kit. We would be able to stay in only a few large hotels where laundry could be done. Modest motels and wayside inns would be fine. We were to learn to perfect a number of useful tricks—such as drying socks in under two minutes, clamped to the business end of an electric hairdryer.

Murray put together and sent packages of maps and guide books to our Consulates in advance, so that we always had what we needed. There was much interest in the possibility of the Rolls breaking down. I had total faith, and much enjoyed assuring those who hoped we would have trouble, that it simply would not happen to a Rolls-Royce. Of course it never did. But we admitted to no one that we did pack a very small spares kit of hoses, belts and the like which Rolls-Royce kindly supplied. Nor did we admit that Murray had some personal training chez Rolls-Royce in fan belt changing—just in case.

Could I afford the time away from the office? One answer was that the car would be a rolling office. We would have two laptop computers—Hilary's with its integral printer, and one with a separate printer from the office, two mobile phones and a satellite telephone on board. The President of the Senate, the Hon. Margaret Reid, warmly recommended carrying a satellite telephone. How right she proved, in one or two entirely unpredictable ways. The telephones enabled me to keep in daily and, when necessary, more frequent touch with the High Commission and Consular Offices. Another answer was that the project had the immediate, enduring and enthusiastic support of my first-rate Deputy High Commissioner, Dr Andrew Pocock. And my Personal Assistant, Ann Douthwaite, was persuaded to join us in Western Australia for five days to help catch up with outstanding work.

Reaction to the plan was rather interesting. The Office in London were a touch cautious; but the 'man on the spot' is there to make such judgments. Among fellow foreign diplomats in Australia there was a mixture of envy, incredulity and a desire to distance themselves from the mad Brits. Official Australians and High Commission and Consular staff were thoroughly supportive. So was the Australia–Britain Society and its admirable National President, Marjorie Turbayne. Lots of people asked to fill the spare seat in the Rolls.

The precise date of the end of our tour, at the mandatory retiring age of 60 for the British Civil Service, presented an obvious timing constraint. Yet we had some flexibility. August was generally quiet in London: it has become increasingly so over the years since we joined the then European Common Market and have become more and more involved as a leading member of the European Union. We seem largely to have adopted the French practice I knew in Paris in the 1960s of limiting government activity as far as possible during the month of August, apparently to enable the Boulevard Périphérique around Paris, and routes south, to be blocked with holiday traffic! There is of course a reciprocal period in Australia, that national holiday which begins before Christmas and ends just after Australia Day, 26 January, and fills the beaches in between.

We were to leave Australia in October, and mid-August to mid-September suited most State governments. It would be a little early for our first stop, in Victoria, but I would in any case need to visit Melbourne again before leaving Australia. Current issues could be dealt with either on the telephone, or by Andrew Pocock. Just a few which might need me to be elsewhere than on the planned route would probably not be critical until our return. In extremis, I could of course fly back to Canberra or to wherever I was needed.

Some advance publicity was carefully organised, and the *Canberra Times* asked if I would write 1000 words a week for the five successive editions of their Sunday newspaper. That was a *new*IMAGE itself: a foreign representative writing what amounted to a weekly column. And that exercise was one of the reasons why I was later encouraged to attempt this book. I never thought I would be writing it, with Hilary as typist, critic and inspiration, during our voyage home aboard a P&O Nedlloyd container ship (the MV *New Zealand Pacific*). Both the opportunity and the ambience were provided by the non-stop passage in November and December, from Port Chalmers in New Zealand across the South Pacific, around Cape Horn and up the Atlantic to Lisbon, en route for London and estimated to arrive there on Christmas Day.

There was a surprising amount of press and television interest. Our departure from Canberra was widely reported, and TV companies covered some parts of the journey in depth—of which much more anon.

Thus the idea of RolleroundOz took shape, form, reason and justification. Hilary invented the idea. Murray was keen. And I was delighted to try a different and new way to pursue British interests in Australia at the end of my tour there. I reflected that Lord Carrington, when High Commissioner in Canberra in the 1950s, had taken the then official Rolls-Royce up the east coast as far as Brisbane, where he and his driver (who still lives in Canberra) decided that that was enough. In the 1970s Sir Donald Tebbit took his Rolls on the ferry to Tasmania. Time and the constraints of other work prevented us from emulating that particular expedition. We travelled separately and later to Hobart and Launceston—of which, also, more later.

RolleroundOz would thus be a first: another reason why we should do it.

1 Canberra to Melbourne

Moments before we left Canberra we enjoyed one of those crisp red dawns of August. The house magpies knocked promptly at the window for their breakfast. Beyond them, the early rays illuminated the flag atop that architectural triumph, Parliament House, and in the other direction the dusting of snow on the Brindabellas' tops. Australia's National Capital at its best.

Our early departure was overseen by Miles and Rachel Warner, the marvellous butler and housekeeper at Westminster House, our official residence. Miles and Rachel, English and Scottish respectively, are now proud new Australians and tremendously efficient and thoughtful professionals. Trained, practised and proficient in hotel management, they ensured, together with Hilary, that Westminster House ran like a Rolls-Royce, with pizzazz and style. In a few years' time, they will, I am sure, be

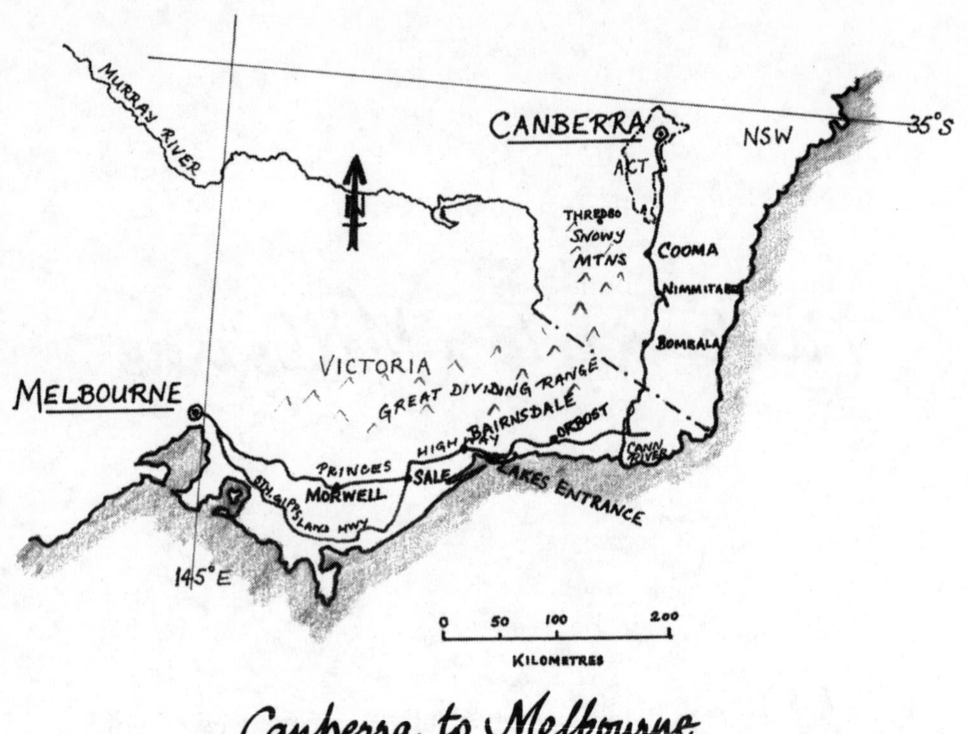

Canberra to Melbourne

running a top-class exclusive Australian hotel with similar style, and with kindness and success. We shall hope to secure a reservation.

We were almost alone, driving past the handsome national buildings and through the Australian Capital Territory to New South Wales, and heading south for the coast. The ACT prohibits advertising hoardings, and they appeared rather suddenly across the NSW border. I thought of Ogden Nash's couplet:

> I think that I shall never see
> A billboard lovely as a tree.

Canberra to Melbourne

As we drove towards the Snowy Mountains, we savoured the morning light through the gum trees and thought it classic Australian artistic inspiration—including perhaps for Arthur Boyd and his tapestry for the Great Hall in Parliament. We had met Arthur Boyd and his wife in their house in Bundanon on New South Wales's south coast, at a pleasant lunch one Saturday for the diplomatic corps, organised, kindly, by the then Australian Foreign Minister Gareth Evans and his wife Merrin. That was the year the Boyds came home for Arthur to be acclaimed of the year. Obviously possessed of huge talent, Arthur is a delight to meet, with his twinkling, almost wicked sense of humour, and a sparkling anti-establishment cast of mind that can be seen so clearly in some of his paintings.

The Bundanon lunch was one of so many memorable occasions we were to recall with pleasure during this tour of Australia. The lunch was memorable also for Gareth's excellent speech, reflecting on seven years as Foreign Minister and delivered with Merrin on his arm, both standing under an inadequate umbrella in the rain. The label on the wine for lunch was signed 'Gordon Bilney', the Minister under Gareth Evans and whose Clare Valley constituency produced some superb wines. This one probably was one such, but we never knew: it threw an ample residue which the off-road journey had stirred into animated suspension. To be rested, not drunk, I thought, but Their Excellencies of the Canberra Corps ensured that not a drop was left.

Back to the road: as we climbed, we slowed for remarkably thick fog, very white and in stark contrast to the brown smogs I recalled from London as a child—smogs happily banished by *Clean Air Acts* while Hilary and I were at school. This morning fog was really one of many clouds hanging in valleys and halo'ed with the now golden rays of the sun. Altogether an inspiring morning to begin a circumnavigation—if that is the right word for a land-based drive around most of the coast of Australia. Circumambulation might be another word but does not suit progress by Rolls-Royce!

We drove through pleasant Cooma, founded in 1849 but probably owing most of its substance to the migrants who came a century later from 27 countries to work on the Snowy Mountains Hydro-Electric Scheme. I was delighted to be able to recall some of the details of the Scheme from having studied it at school in England in the early 1950s, when the sheer engineering brilliance and imaginative audacity of concept and design fired Britain and the world with enthusiasm and respect.

Cooma was also distinguished that morning by colossal cavalcades of sulphur-crested cockatoos. We hoped that they would recruit more from the garden of the High Commission Residence in Canberra, where a battalion or so wreaked daily damage and filled the dusk with demonic squawking.

The Rolls-Royce's outside temperature gauge and ice warning indicator confirmed the frostiness of the fields and explained why the cows and sheep were looking distinctly downcast.

As we skirted the Snowy Mountains, we thought sad thoughts of Thredbo where Hilary and I had had happy times and where, a little before we began our journey, that dreadful landslide had caused terrible tragedy, trapping and killing people inside collapsed buildings. Just one miraculous rescue had been achieved in an heroic battle against a concentrated, cruel stroke of nature. One of the staff in the Consular Section of the High Commission and her husband were part of the rescue team. Much later, I learned much from a sobering conversation with that admirable young lady. Australians, and many of the rest of us, will never forget Thredbo. It will be important to visit again. I was glad to think that a British Armed Services team of skiers would soon be competing there.

We pressed on through rolling open country. The predominant colours were gold and green—as we were to see so often around this vast continent of a country. No wonder that Australian national sporting teams wear these colours. We purred on towards the coast and began to be cheered again by the freshness of the morning and the gentle attractiveness of the countryside. The quiet was a joy, too, and I thought of the old story of the advertising line that the loudest sound in a Rolls-Royce at 60 miles an hour was the ticking of the electric clock. A modern Australian truth suddenly became abundantly clear: the loudest sound in a Rolls-Royce in New South Wales that morning at 100 km an hour was the uproarious laughter of a pair of kookaburras on a telegraph wire at twenty paces.

It took almost no time to drive through a small town, Nimmitabel, but we all noticed the immaculate Remembrance Garden and War Memorial. We would certainly see many more of these throughout this country which honours its war dead with such dignity, style and meaning.

I grew up during and after World War II, and knew that we in Britain performed this particular exercise in gratitude and respect to those to whom we owed everything better than any other country did. My National Service in the Royal Navy confirmed this conviction. Later, as I moved around the world, I met others who believed the same of their countries. I thought them all wrong…until I served in Australia. We talked in the car about this, and about that fine year-long exercise during the 50th anniversary end of World War II commemorations, Australia Remembers.

That was a deeply impressive and sustained effort in expressing obligation and gratitude, and in educating the young. I believe Britain's commemorations—for example, D-Day, VE-Day and VJ-Day—were of world-wide importance, and were expressions of solemn ceremonial and renewed commemoration of the highest order. But the depth, breadth and length of Australia Remembers, and its impact throughout the land and among the very young as well as the very old, were extraordinary and second to none. I was glad that the UK and the British Armed Services had been able to play some small part in Australia Remembers, by way of parades, exhibitions and other events. Few of those present will forget the Beating of the Retreat in the Residence garden at night by the Pipes and Drums of the First Battalion of the King's Own Scottish Borderers—and not only because it poured with rain throughout their Sunset Ceremony, their marching, drumming, sword dancing and bagpiping, all of which caused one ex-Scottish Australian, our splendid doctor Tom Middlemiss, who had not been back to Scotland in some 30 years, to say unconvincingly as he took his leave, 'I'm not home-sick, I'm not home-sick...!'

And the black and white photographic exhibition with captions and commentaries, whose accuracy was rigorously checked by military historians, illustrated to good effect the British role in the Far East and the Pacific in World War II. We covered much of Australia by moving around fifteen copies of that exhibition. It set the record straight on what we had and hadn't done in Singapore. It described some of the Royal Air Force's contributions alongside the Royal Australian Air Force in the defence of Darwin. It reminded us how Bill Slim's army had held down 385 000 Japanese troops for nearly three and a half years in Burma, thus preventing their being deployed, perhaps for invasion of even more strategically precious parts of this region. And it illustrated the extraordinary recovery of the Royal Navy and its contribution of over 600 ships and many thousands of men in the Far East and the Pacific.

Robert Ray, then Australian Minister of Defence, opened the exhibition in Canberra, and spoke authoritatively and appreciatively; and I was particularly glad to learn that Paul Keating went to see it privately. (More of Paul Keating later.) Robert Ray was a refreshingly straight and able minister for a foreign diplomat to deal with. He has a sense of humour as arid as the Gibson Desert. A senior Rolls-Royce (Aerospace) marketing man went to call on him wearing a fashionable tie covered in rows of ducks. Robert sat silent and expressionless through ten minutes of mellifluous spiel on the qualities of the Rolls-Royce Adour jet-engine and then said, 'I do like your

English cricket tie.' Collapse of Rolls-Royce Aerospace executive.

One of the unexpected advantages of RolleroundOz, we were to find, was the inspiration of and opportunity for reflections such as these: not only of the preceding three years or so Hilary and I had spent so happily in Australia, but also of UK–Australian history—colonial, military, economic and financial, cultural, scientific, people-to-people and political. Wordsworth defined poetry as emotion recollected in tranquillity. The emotion of enjoying the vastness and drama of the Australian countryside, and the tranquillity of thus experiencing it, were to lend enchantment and objectivity to the view of all these elements of the UK–Australian relationship. It had a little to do with being away from the pressures of the desk, a lot to do with the grandeur, the beauty and, so often, the emptiness of Australia.

But it was my turn to drive. We passed through Bombala, which looks a little like a film set for a western. As we approached the State of Victoria, the land seemed to grow greener in patches. And it was still cold. The sheep were wearing plastic coats—or were they mackintoshes? They were colourful too: we hoped it was a matter of fashion rather than colour coding. The horses had blankets. The old wooden bridges lay woebegone and unused beside new spans of concrete. On a few kilometres of hilly gravel road we stopped to enjoy the company of two velvet black wallabies and two wombats who performed elegantly and apparently professionally for Hilary's video camera (of which more anon). And hereabouts the wattles were blooming: the first of many varieties we saw.

Altogether, our first morning on the road was thoroughly uplifting to the spirit.

Hilary was driving as we reached Lakes Entrance, an enchanting harbour. I greatly enjoyed the rows of fine fishing boats, and one lovely motor-sailer schooner, which made me wonder whether it were engaged in a more literal circumnavigation of Australia than ours. We stopped to watch dredging at the entrance to Lakes Entrance from some way up the nearby hill. A fascinating sight, because looking down through the clear water it was easy to see the unremitting silting and how essential the constant dredging is to the continued usefulness and, indeed, existence of the harbour.

By now it was working hours in Canberra so I tested the satellite phone. It worked very well, and enabled some necessary work to be done efficiently. As I reported later to the *Canberra Times* for the Sunday edition, I concluded that one can both be High Commissioner and travel—provided that there is a first class Deputy, PA and staff. As I also reported, I began to relax.

Hilary drove us into Bairnsdale, and found a family restaurant for lunch. What a contrast with The Lobby restaurant in Canberra, or the dining room in Westminster House. The chat at tables in Bairnsdale was happy enough and animated, but had no political content whatsoever. It was easy to relax further. Hilary was to keep a careful account of expenses throughout our journey. She requested a receipt when we paid. The waitress, in her late teens, her hair a touch awry, reflecting perhaps the rush of Bairnsdale lunch-time customers, said this was no worry at all. But she had a new experience that day: the treasure hunt for the ancient receipt book was a long and detailed affair. Finally discovered, the book looked as if it had been used three times since it was new—all in the year 1910. Then began a second leisurely hunt, for the carbon paper. Later, the pencil needed sharpening…We relaxed even more.

We had driven from Canberra to Melbourne twice before when taking the Rolls-Royce to the Melbourne Cup—to go with Hilary's hats and the tails and topper. But we had never seen green, fertile and hugely attractive Latrobe Valley and Gippsland. The eucalyptus trees were majestic and the wattle was glorious. Wombats grazed on the edge of the road. Rich farming country abounded in Devonian green pastures, complete with Friesian cows and their calves. Murray has much country experience and pointed out one uncomfortable looking cow who, he told us, was about to give birth. We were glad it was now the warmest part of the day!

Sale is a large sprawling town we found notable for its substantial churches and some handsome old buildings with wrought iron. We have always much enjoyed the wrought iron lace-work on houses in the older established towns in Australia, and admired the combination of imagination and pragmatism of designing and using wrought iron first as ballast in ships sailing from the UK to Australia and, after arrival, for decorative domestic effect.

Between rain showers—some of the very few we were to experience in 17 400 km driving around Australia—we enjoyed the Dandenongs, and later the Yarra Range, particularly for their compelling eucalyptus-vapour blue which contrasted with the streaks of snow. And we reflected that all we had seen so far was readily accessible from Canberra, if only one gets out of bed early.

The rain caused us to alter our planned route (a trick Hilary and I had learned many years earlier driving two young boys and a dog around England one summer holiday). We were impressed by the mine at Morwell, and by its attendant power stations. Escaping the rain, we enjoyed further profusion of wattles, crossed countless railway level crossings and began finally to enter ribbon development and suburban Melbourne.

The car, or mobile, or satellite telephone—one of them at any rate—rang with news that an ABC TV team would like to join us at breakfast the next day and take some film over the following few days. Agreed.

In Melbourne we stayed, as nearly always, in the British Consul-General's Residence guest suite. This is a happy arrangement, and the Consul-General and his wife, George and Pat Finlayson, are old and good friends. George is now British High Commissioner to Malawi.

We must have been to Melbourne 30 or 40 times in the last three and a bit years. It has of course a distinctly European feel, and the sophisticated business, political, artistic and other communities are a guarantee that we always have an enjoyable and productive time. There seems to be a ready acceptance of most things British—cricket of course being an exception, save that we have been welcome in recent years because we have been relatively easy to beat (that shall change!).

It was during our second visit to Melbourne that a senior Australian businessman told me that he was prepared to do business with Brits on a handshake—only

High Commissions and Consulates

While foreign countries exchange Ambassadors, member countries of the Commonwealth exchange High Commissioners. Like other Commonwealth countries represented in Australia then, Britain has a High Commission in Canberra. Britain also has six subordinate posts around Australia. In RolleroundOz order, these are in Melbourne, Adelaide, Perth, Brisbane, Sydney and Hobart. Adelaide, a small Consulate, and Hobart, an Honorary Consulate, are hierarchically subordinate initially to Melbourne which, with the others, is a Consulate-General. All are predominantly trade offices, and Sydney has responsibility for co-ordination and direction of this work, under the High Commission. UK-based diplomats run the Consulates-General. Of all foreign and Commonwealth Missions in Australia, the UK has the most extensive network of diplomatic/consular posts. That is hardly surprising, given the depth, extent and further potential of the relationship between the two countries and the work all that involves.

with Brits. I have since come across or experienced a number of examples of this, including seriously large deals. And politics in Melbourne are fun, particularly I suppose for the disinterested diplomatic observer. When I first met the Premier of Victoria, Jeff Kennett, he told me horror stories of his years in opposition, and fun stories of making things work in power. When we went with Lady Thatcher to have dinner with him high above the city. We had a marvellous view, including of the pouring rain. Jeff proudly showed us Melbourne, and explained 'we're just washing her down'. I shall long remember Jeff's masterly defence of government involvement in casinos over dinner that evening with Margaret Thatcher, who expressed the opposing view with her customary vigour and conviction.

We have done much good UK–Victoria business in recent years, and Jeff Kennett has been supportive. He also gave me the right tip for the 1994 Melbourne Cup, though he failed to back that horse himself. The next time I called on him, he was sporting a smart bright tie with jockey colours all over it. He accepted my compliment upon it and then described my admittedly boring civil servant's striped tie as 'bloody awful'. I had to agree. Later that morning I changed it and sent the boring one to him with a note saying that clearly I could never wear it again: perhaps he would like to, or to donate it to the nearest blind school. He responded with a note saying that he was shattered and I naked, and enclosed a new tie. Clearly I could never wear that one either: it was the tie of his own political party. However I did wear it on my farewell call on Jeff Kennett.

As a British diplomat, I have also much enjoyed the rivalry in so much between Melbourne and Sydney. It is an understandable but nonetheless extraordinary feature of Australian life. Also understandably, for many years the healthy rivalry has been reflected in relations between the two British (and perhaps other?) Consulates-General. I saw it first in the early 1980s but I am told it existed long before. The one, for example, claims that 'his' parish is the more populous, the other that he covers three States. Consuls-General in Perth and Brisbane have other impressive measures, of course. But most fun can be had explaining to Sydney-siders the advantages of Melbourne and vice versa. Perhaps the best rejoinder I have heard from a Melburnian about Sydney's attractions is that the real trouble with Sydney is that it is too far out of town.

Melbourne and Victoria will indeed figure large in our memories. We took a visiting British minister there after I had been High Commissioner only two days, and learned a great deal, including from members of that impressive collection of heavy hitters, the Committee for Melbourne. Hilary and I have been there with two Lord Mayors of London. At the Melbourne Cup we have enjoyed the company of that shrewd Aussie observer of the British scene Clive James, and of such fans of Melbourne and of Australia as Derek Nimmo and Lynne Redgrave—whose performance of her tribute to her father Michael was easily the best one-person (to be politically correct) show we have ever seen: it is a pity only that while Lynne felt entirely happy about performing this fine, tender, respectful, funny and altogether admirable work of hers in Australia, she never felt the same about doing so in England.

Melbourne has been a welcoming host to a number of British *new*IMAGES events. '*new*IMAGES' because we felt that despite the objectively impressive facts and figures of the commercial, economic, political and cultural relationships between Australia and Britain, the relationship was vulnerable to hurt because of misperceptions by so many people in each country of the other. In part, the misperceptions are a function of the success of contemporary exchange in the field of entertainment. I often jest that *Neighbours*, that run-away television success exported from Australia to the UK, must be widely regarded among my countrymen and women as a documentary, so deeply do they seem to believe it a precise and accurate reflection of the Australian way of life. And as a British civil servant I am increasingly presented with evidence that Australians regard *Yes Minister* as another of those masterly BBC documentaries. (And I am devoutly grateful that my parents did not choose the name Humphrey for me!)

The results of surveys by both the Australian High Commission in London and by ourselves here in Australia of attitudes to the other country were both amusing and disturbing. Some of the less than flattering and less than accurate views found in Australia about Poms might just, I suppose, have been purveyed by British immigrants here—perhaps in some attempt to excuse the act of emigration (the UK is still today a major source of immigrants to Australia). And the fact that new pubs in London make good money by being decorated as 'Australian'—with surfboards swinging from the ceiling and road signs pointing to Earls Court—has its worrying implications. The information media, the very clever Les Patterson and other influences are not always objective, inevitably.

While Australia vies with France and Germany to be the third largest external investor in the UK; while the UK lies a close second to the USA as the largest external investor in Australia, way above Japan; and while trade between us exceeds $A13 billion a year, I believe both that we could do much better and that the future of the relationship would be better assured and still more mutually beneficial if the risks implicit in outdated and inaccurate images in each country of the other, and the risk of negative comment at the tabloid level based on these misperceptions, could be removed, or at least minimised.

This view was quite widely held: hence *new*IMAGES, for which the British Foreign Secretary at the time of inception and decision, Douglas Hurd, who had visited Australia and formed his own clear view, should take the credit. Melbourne saw a good deal of *new*IMAGES: exhibitions and theatre events—including the Royal Shakespeare Company's stunningly innovative production of a *Midsummer Night's Dream*—a new image of its own which was a brilliant artistic success elsewhere in Australia too. Melbourne also had sculpture on Herring Island, exhibitions and a range of hard-nosed commercial events, all culminating in 'UK Now', a $A2.5 million-plus multifaceted event opened by Margaret Beckett, President of the Board of Trade and Secretary of State for Trade and Industry in late November 1997, after we had left—a fine early event for my fortunate successor, Alex Allan. Melbourne-based businesses were notably responsive and generous sponsors and supporters of *new*IMAGES. I am sure they will also have gained much from their investment.

Hilary and I have known, and profited from knowing, two Governors of Victoria. Both the McGarvies and the Gobbos have been most hospitable. Discussion with Governor McGarvie revealed that he was concerned that there was insufficient knowledge among Australians about their Constitution. He wrote excellent learned papers and, after retirement as Governor, addressed the issues more publicly, and to good effect. The farewell lunch the McGarvies' successors gave us included a rare treat, 'black' asparagus, presented to Lady Gobbo by the horticulturalist who had perfected it. But it was the conversation at the lunch which readily persuaded me that Sir James Gobbo, another distinguished judge, would also make his mark.

I have enjoyed the company of each of the governors at the top table of one of the more extraordinary and distinguished Scottish organisations I have known around the world, the Melbourne Scots. It is a particular and welcome privilege to be invited to the Melbourne Scots St Andrew's Day Dinner; and even more so to be invited to address nearly 400 kilted or black-tied distinguished men, the denizens of the Caledonian Antipodes. The attention to correct Scottish ceremonial is complete. The enjoyment of the evening expands exponentially with the ceremonial, the community activities and the entire Hawthorn Pipe Band, whose delightful Drum Major, Bob Semple, I first met at the Java St Andrew's Society's Highland Gathering in Jakarta, and who kindly kept me supplied with programmes of that, the largest Highland Gathering in the Southern Hemisphere (there's a challenge for Australian Scots!). Enjoyment also increases at the St Andrew's Dinner with the speeches, provided they are sophisticated and funny: the audience can be more demanding than any at the Glasgow Empire! And the conversation is always both profound and brilliant. How could it be otherwise when those at the table, under the guise of President, Chieftain, guests and officers, included such Australian greats as Sir Ninian Stephen, Malcolm Fraser, Sir Zelman

Cowen, successive governors of Victoria, leading corporate Victorians such as Don Mercer, former Premier Sir Rupert Hamer and many others. Great men and good.

I must briefly pay particular tribute to Sir Zelman Cowen of whom I have seen most among those just named. Sir Zelman has of course many connections with the UK and he has been a quite wonderful and unstintingly generous source of wise advice, of philosophic illumination and, with Anna, of sheer personal kindness. He also gave his name to a flagship British Government annual scholarship.

Given that on our journey around Australia, the next State capital after Melbourne is Adelaide, one must say something about the Grand Prix! We have enjoyed it in both State capitals and, again, found it an occasion on which to do diplomatic business—commercial and political. It was fun, again as an impartial observer, to watch the battle and to commiserate with the one and congratulate the other as the Australian Grand Prix moved from Adelaide to Melbourne—or should I say from 'Sensational Adelaide' to the 'world's most livable city'. We have friends in each of these two cities who go away for the weekend of the Grand Prix. But the Grand Prix is certainly special. My status as an impartial observer collapsed when Brit Damon Hill won the last Grand Prix in Adelaide—and was a popular winner there too. And my impartial observer status suffered a further severe blow when British Aerospace Australia was such a formidable and foremost sponsor at the Melbourne Grand Prix of 1997—the year the RAAF selected an advanced version of the BAe Hawk for their lead-in fighter trainer (complete with Rolls-Royce Adour engines!).

Canberra to Melbourne

There is so much to say, and to enjoy, about Melbourne: its restaurants, environs, architectural development (most of it), historic public buildings, neighbourhoods, sporting prowess, quirks (the Range Rover or 'Toorak Tractor', never leaving the bitumen, is one such), its trams, 'hook-left' turns, its—and Victoria's —economic recovery (Treasurer Alan Stockdale take a deep bow), its upside-down river, culture and arts, academic and medical excellence, the charities and their devoted and energetic supporters, the distinguished clubs, not excluding the nearby, unique and excellent West Brighton Club (whose dinners are extraordinary and wondrous affairs), the harbour, the Melbourne Cricket Ground, the business people, people in general and in particular, but not, perhaps, or not always, Melbourne's weather (though that too shall change, probably twice in the next hour).

2 Melbourne to Ceduna

Our second day started with a working breakfast with the Consul-General, whose other guest was Professor Ian Wallace, Vice-Chancellor of Swinburne University. With the help of Sheila Bramley of the High Commission, Consul-General George had been negotiating with Swinburne over the details of a joint British Government and Swinburne University post-graduate annual scholarship to the UK. This breakfast was to sign the resulting agreement, and to talk about its implementation. Richard Pratt, senior Melbourne-based international businessman, investor in the UK and Chancellor of Swinburne University and, with his wife, supporter of the arts, had played a key part in establishing the scholarship. Such joint efforts are obviously beneficial to the winner of the scholarship and to both countries, and have much potential for further developing contacts and relations between the two countries in the most important area of all: the future.

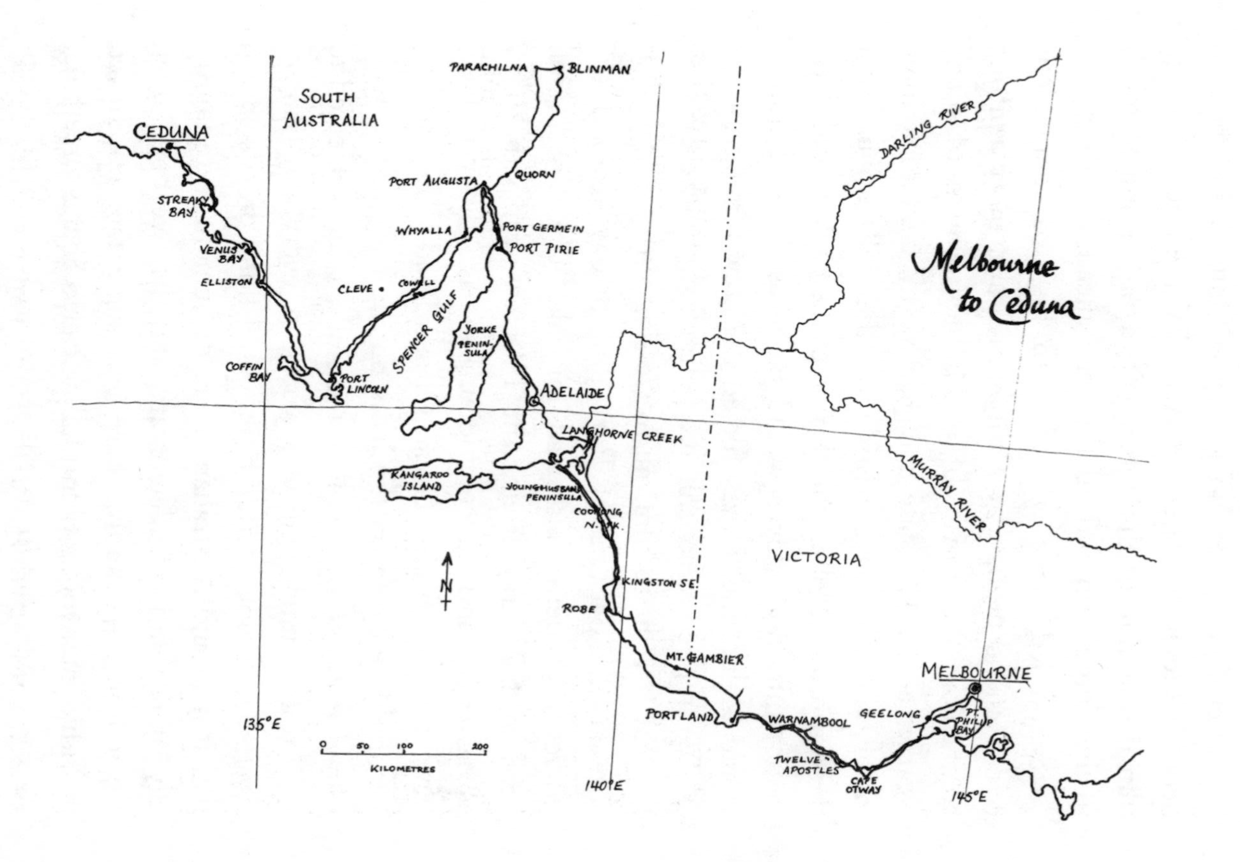
Melbourne to Ceduna
CEDUNA
SOUTH AUSTRALIA
STREAKY BAY
VENUS BAY
ELLISTON
COFFIN BAY
PORT LINCOLN
CLEVE
COWELL
SPENCER GULF
WHYALLA
PORT AUGUSTA
QUORN
PARACHILNA
BLINMAN
PORT GERMEIN
PORT PIRIE
YORKE PENINSULA
ADELAIDE
LANGHORNE CREEK
KANGAROO ISLAND
YOUNGHUSBAND PENINSULA
KINGSTON SE.
ROBE
MT. GAMBIER
PORTLAND
VICTORIA
WARNAMBOOL
TWELVE APOSTLES
CAPE OTWAY
GEELONG
PT. PHILLIP BAY
MELBOURNE
DARLING RIVER
MURRAY RIVER
N
135°E
140°E
145°E
0 50 100 200
KILOMETRES

An unscheduled subject for an erudite and entertaining discussion at breakfast turned out to be modern Scottish literature. Then an ABC TV crew joined us to film the signing of the agreement, as a prelude to much further filming on and off the road ahead.

Simon led the crew and, with his two companions (video and sound), was a thoughtful and most amusing companion. We drove out of Melbourne in mild sunny weather across Westgate Bridge. The TV crew took some imaginative film on the bridge of the Rolls driving past the downtown Melbourne skyline in the background. Dramatic stuff. Rolls-Royce would be pleased. So, I hoped, would Melbourne. Hilary filmed the crew filming us.

We stopped to consult at a petrol station, where Simon thought it right to film me expressing surprise and pleasure at the packets of Port Phillip Bay seafood the purveyor of petrol also had for sale. The consultation resulted in Murray driving the TV crew's car with Hilary as passenger, and the crew joining me as I drove to Geelong and on to the Great Ocean Road. The camera, apparently focused on the hairs on the back of my neck, filmed from the back seat of the Rolls. I was subjected to a distinctly intelligent viva voce on everything Anglo-Australian Simon's fertile brain could think of. We agreed that British and Australian senses of humour were unusually similar and complementary, and that we both much enjoy irony. Inevitably, there was some talk of cricket, including of a young blond fellow called Shane something. As we stopped again to enable the ABC crew to recapture their motor car, Simon said how much he had enjoyed the ride in the Rolls: he had not felt, he said, as if he were in a car at all.

Beyond Geelong, an unmarked police car pulled over an unsuspecting speedster. As the driver got out of his car, he pulled on a police baseball cap by way of identification, if not intimidation. I suppose it was fair warning rather than intimidation that lay behind the sign at the entrance to Surfers' Beach. It read 'Back Street Booze Patrols Working'! I wondered if drivers who had imbibed therefore stuck to the main streets, and who was bluffing whom.

The Great Ocean Road was built after World War I by returning soldiers as a memorial to those they had left behind. We had driven the Great Ocean Road once before, but in the other direction. I now warmly recommend doing it both ways, for two different but equally superb views. For Hilary and me, the road recalled Route 1 in California, the coast road between San Francisco and Los Angeles. We enjoyed finding similarities and differences. One difference was that here in Victoria, the gale-blown spray leapt above the highest cliffs. Another was Wattle Hill, which despite the drizzle was liberal with much bright promise of spring—although even that recalled the yellow mimosa trees around San Francisco. A third difference was the rainforest area of the Great Ocean Road. The similarities, of winding steep roads with sudden spectacular sweeping coastline views, frequently recur; but nowhere else has the Twelve Apostles.

I recalled another time I had seen these skyscraper limestone pinnacles, once part of the cliffs of this wreck-ridden Victorian coastline. That was at sunset, flying in a light aeroplane a few hundred feet above the Twelve Apostles with the sun dipping into the sea behind us. It was one of those memories to be enjoyed for ever. The occasion was a return flight to Melbourne from a duty engagement helping the Deputy Premier of Victoria to open the Mary Rose Exhibition in Warrnambool. Pat McNamara is a gentlemanly, relaxed and astute politician. I think he will never forget that flight either. I recalled, too, the pilot of that same small aeroplane saying how on another occasion he had answered a question from the Premier, Jeff Kennett, as to how long another flight would take. 'Roughly an hour' was the answer. 'No,' said Jeff: 'Smoothly an hour!'

We stopped for lunch with the crew at Lorne, in a pub with a view for which real estate people would kill. The crew's mobile phones rang more often than ours. The fine weather had closed in rather, and was clearly going to worsen. That forecast, and a telephone conference about it, spelled the end of a plan to film the Rolls driving on the Great Ocean Road from a helicopter. Despite their disappointment, or perhaps because of it, the crew did an excellent job of filming from their car, from the Rolls-Royce and from well-selected vantage points. Again, Hilary filmed them, and added to our unique record.

For one stage of the Great Ocean Road, and with our agreement, the crew had bugged the Rolls and monitored it from their following car. But they heard nothing exciting or useable, as they told us to their chagrin when they later removed the microphone. They did not know that Hilary and I had spent three years driving in bugged cars when serving behind the Iron Curtain in the depths of the

Cold War. We slipped back with barely an effort into the habit, finely tuned in communist Bulgaria, of talking amusedly without revealing anything of interest at all!

When the crew left us to return to Melbourne, the two cars pulled off the road, and we jumped out on to verdant springy grass at the top of a cliff with one of those fabulous views. We parted good friends with the ABC, with Simon and his colleagues, and should much like to meet them again. We would meet another of Simon's colleagues and his crew the following day in South Australia.

As the Great Ocean Road ends, Route 100 leads through the Otway National Park. We much enjoyed the beech forest but sadly had no time to divert to Cape Otway itself. We recalled the story of the *Cataraqui*, a ship which sailed from Liverpool to Australia with settlers in 1845; a ship whose eventual wreck was to be Australia's biggest civilian maritime disaster. It remains so to this day. The story has a little to do with Cape Otway. A well researched and thorough book on the subject has been produced, but here, briefly, is my own recollection of how I heard the tale of woe.

Over 150 years ago, in villages in Oxfordshire and Shropshire in England and County Antrim in Ireland, Parish Church Council Treasurers were alarmed at the cost of supporting the poor. They proposed providing poor families with a coat or blanket for each member and despatching them by horse-drawn cart to Liverpool where a ship, the *Cataraqui*, would convey them to the land of golden opportunity, Australia. There was little argument around the Council tables. The *Cataraqui* assembled her crew and her human cargo. There was some evidence of a feud between the captain and the ship's surgeon. There was good evidence that the mate was an especially fine sailor. Four hundred and nine souls, some 50 of them crew, were crammed aboard the *Cataraqui*, probably a ship-rigged vessel, although some say a barque, not much larger than Captain Cook's barque *Endeavour*.

The *Cataraqui* sailed south from Liverpool, around the Cape of Good Hope and eastwards to Australia. One black night, 122 days after leaving Liverpool, and eight days after the last fix on the chart by sextant (the last because the sun had not been seen since), the captain was on deck in a severe gale. All sail had been furled: the *Cataraqui* was hove-to under bare poles. By one account the captain and the surgeon had an altercation on deck. At all events, the captain believed his ship was off Cape Otway, and safely so. The mate, off watch and asleep below, stirred and awoke quickly as he became aware of a change in the ship's motion which could be explained only by some sail having been hoisted. Alarmed, the mate ran up on to the deck, to find some sail hoisted and straining at the westerly gale—and the captain in charge. Such was the discipline of the day that the mate retired below again, silent.

Shortly afterwards, the *Cataraqui* hit a rocky shore, hard. But she clawed off again. Ten minutes later she hit again, further along the shore. This time, sharp jagged rocks bit deeper, and captured and held her.

But it was not Cape Otway. The rocks were part of King Island, some 70 nautical miles to the south. Boats were launched and immediately dashed to pieces on the jagged rocks around the ship. The families of would-be settlers from inland Britain, many of whom could never have seen the sea, much less have been able to swim, suffered a cruel death at the hands of the sea and the rocks. Some of the experienced crew lashed themselves to the stronger parts of the ship. Those who did so at the forepeak did better than the others. Of the 409 men, women and children who left Liverpool aboard the *Cataraqui*, nine men survived. Of those, one was an aspirant settler (who lost sixteen members of his family), and eight were crew—including the mate. The captain, the surgeon and all others perished.

King Island was virtually uninhabited at the time, save for a small group of Aboriginal women who hunted seal which they sold to a Melbourne trader. A few days later the gale subsided and the trader made a delayed visit to the island to collect the seal skins. The Aborigines told him of a disaster on the western side of the Island. With his colleagues he found bodies spread three miles up and down the coast, and the few survivors. Together they did their best to provide decent burial and then sailed back to Melbourne, where the mate and others made depositions to the court.

One hundred and fifty years later King Island mounted a commemoration of the loss of the *Cataraqui*, and invited Hilary and me to take part. The wreck, after all, was Britain's fault, and I was the British High Commissioner. The Island put on an extraordinary and unforgettable series of events, of which the centrepiece was the dedication of a cairn on the beach just inshore from the rocks on which the *Cataraqui* was wrecked, and near the place where the archaeologists had recently established that some 270 of the 400 dead had been buried.

The hunt for the burial ground had taken some years, and involved modern search techniques. It was aided too by a transparency of an early Tasmanian bishop's sketch showing jagged rocks and a (long gone) picket fence apparently around the rough graves. The archaeologist walked the shore with the transparency until he found the rocks which fitted it: they did so exactly.

The dedication service must be an indelible memory to all who took part, from the bishop and leaders of other churches who came from Tasmania, to the children of King Island who sang the hymns to the music of the brass band and who had completed many projects about the *Cataraqui*. Then there were the Lions Club whose impressive undertaking this was, the television film crew and other visitors, and apparently most of the leaders and members of the population of King Island. As I read an Old Testament lesson, appropriately enough in a gale of wind, a fishing boat wrestled up and down with the waves, just beyond those jagged rocks, to signal the ghostly presence of the *Cataraqui*. A descendant of a Cornish seaman, one of the survivors, who now produced wine in Victoria, spoke movingly—until he was too moved to continue.

We pressed on, reluctantly leaving the thrilling Great Ocean Road, to Warrnambool. Running late now, we had to miss an intended visit to the Maritime Museum there, which I much regret. We did have a quick look at Portland, a pleasant little port with some good-looking yachts and a handsome hotel with that wrought iron lace-work again. We crossed into South Australia and adjusted our watches and the Rolls's clock. One day that process too will be automatic, by low frequency radio control.

We reached Mount Gambier, our overnight stop, an hour after sundown. So next day we started at dawn to see the town's surprising volcanic lakes before pressing on towards the coast again. We drove through timberlands, then rich pastures and flatter land where tea-trees dominated delightfully. Two black swans flew past going the other way. We spoke of the first black swans in England which were an Australian gift to Winston Churchill for his country house at Chartwell. We thought it must have been Bob Menzies who made that gift. We stopped at Robe, which has a purposeful, quiet harbour, and an interesting history of Chinese workers landing here on their way to the goldfields at Ballarat. Financially astute as ever, the Chinese knew that if they landed conveniently close to Ballarat in Victoria, they would have to pay State taxes which South Australia did not levy. The Chinese had to tramp, however, some 400 km from Robe to Ballarat. Tramp they did, some pushing wheelbarrows, the story goes. We could not help wondering what landing charges they paid in Robe, and how far they were told it was to Ballarat.

Back to modern Australia: we listened on the car radio to an interview in Mount Gambier with John Olsen, Premier of South Australia. The issues were fiercely local, but it was interesting to hear how well-briefed the Premier evidently was, and how much he was master of his brief. He argued Mount Gambier issues as if he had lived there all his life, and seemed to me to win the encounter with the able and also well-briefed radio journalist.

We drove on, the 6.7 litre Rolls-Royce engine happily purring, to Kingston, to its lighthouse, the Norfolk pines along the beach front, the 1867 Bank and the venerable hotel The Royal Mail. Between there and the Coorong National Park and on to Meningie, some of the scenery reminded us of the Fens in England. And we enjoyed the Coorong's lagoon—over 100 km long but never more than 3 km wide, sheltered by the sand dunes of the Younghusband Peninsula—and the resident cormorants, pelicans and ibises.

We turned north to skirt Lakes Albert and Alexandrina at the end of the massive Murray River system, which I studied at school in England in 1949 and can still draw—just. A nesting magpie near the river confirmed the early spring we were now much enjoying. The distance since Mount Gambier seemed huge, and we were days from beginning the Nullarbor!

By arrangement on the telephone, we met another able and pleasant ABC TV crew at Wellington, a little ferry crossing on the Murray. The ferry took the Rolls plus one, and made good video. We drove on to Langhorne Creek for lunch at the warmly welcoming Bridge Hotel. Here we did some more filming, including of interesting chat with customers in the pub about the North-West Shelf and mining management; and with smiling landlord and former schoolmaster Tom Bauerochse about local history, floods and their management for irrigation of the important grape production of Langhorne Creek. We also filmed interviews, including one with Murray while he assiduously polished the Spirit of Ecstasy atop the Rolls's bonnet. This was an entertaining and interesting interlude.

We all enjoyed Tom's company greatly. He asked me if I would swap the Rolls for his pub. I said I might take the pub as a deposit! Tom was a mine of fascinating facts about Langhorne Creek, and his two mining customers were forthcoming and friendly. One worked off-shore to save and invest capital: he was in the process of buying a newsagency in Tailem Bend.

I knew Foreign Minister Alexander Downer's constituency was hereabouts, but I did not know it included Langhorne Creek until he told me so after he had seen the ABC's film report of RolleroundOz. Alexander was the second Australian Federal Minister in the Department of Foreign Affairs and Trade I had known with a wine-growing South Australian constituency (Gordon Bilney was the other). I had most to do with Alexander Downer, whom I first met properly at the Adelaide Oval (of which more anon). As Foreign Minister, Alexander was both hospitable and helpful in South Australia over what we agreed was an overlapping Australia–UK interest. This was one reason for happy memories as we drove on through the lovely Adelaide Hills. There was another, also with a wine connection: Nicky Downer, Alexander's English-born wife, used to play a key role in the Barossa Music Festival, and persuaded us to stimulate a British contribution to it. We had become admirers both of the Festival and of the wine of the Barossa ever since we first stocked the cellar at Westminster House largely from the Barossa Valley. Early in our posting in Australia, Murray had driven the Rolls's predecessor, a Silver Spur II, laden with Barossa wine, back to Canberra.

There is, too, a story I like about Gordon Bilney.

Australian Wine

Wine has been produced in Australia for 200 years. Countless Londoners—and I—first knew of Australian wine some years ago as Chateau Collapseau (or Cardboard), the clever Australian invention of bag and tap in cardboard case. It is a tribute to Australia's modern, hygienic, intelligent viticulture that its high quality wine has leapt early marketing obstacles and commands serious international respect and market share. Our own favourites come from South Australia (where over 60 per cent of Australia's wine is produced); but Victoria, where the Yarra Valley, for example, shines with noble varieties, Margaret River in Western Australia with wines of great refinement and excellence—including on the Leeuwin Estate where open air concerts are also rightly acclaimed, and of course the Hunter Valley of NSW are all major players. Caveat potor!

Gordon had one of the smallest electoral majorities in the Federal Parliament in which he served, so he had to nurse his McLaren Vale constituency. He has a quick and sometimes quirky sense of humour, and when O. J. Simpson was found not guilty of murdering his wife in that famous and very public trial in the USA, closely followed on television in Australia as elsewhere, Gordon acted fast. Within a few hours a poster was seen throughout his constituency, it seemed almost on every tree. In three well-designed sections, the poster declared at the top 'O.J. Simpson is innocent!'. The second section read 'And

I'm Kylie Minogue'. The third section was signed 'Gordon Bilney'.

On through the Adelaide Hills: we enjoyed and admired again the wire mesh straps thoughtfully fitted at intervals over the concrete median barrier to help koalas cross the road. Down into the city of churches we drove, for some preparatory work for the following day of official calls and a speech, and then for a relaxed and enjoyable farewell dinner at the Adelaide Club given by the former Honorary Consul-General, John Morphett CBE, and his wife Vivienne, and in the company also of the present full-time Consul and his wife, Vic and Fran Warrington.

Next day we called on the South Australia Governor, Sir Eric Neal, and Lady Neal (who were also to help with a *new*IMAGES project for schoolchildren). The Governor conveys his thoughtful observations in a friendly, effective way. He achieves the remarkable feat of successfully following Dame Roma Mitchell, in part by being so different from Dame Roma, an immensely experienced and widely loved former judge. For an engineer and businessman, charitable to boot, Sir Eric is also a remarkable historian of South Australia.

At the Australia–Britain Chamber of Commerce (ABCC) Awards lunch in Adelaide, Premier John Olsen, in his usual fine style, and unprompted, delivered some *new*IMAGES messages related to current Australia–UK business, and opportunities for more, including at and after INFORM 97, an international information technology exhibition in Adelaide, where the UK presence was strong and productive. Parts of John Olsen's speech could almost have been written by the Brits, which illustrated the commonality of need and purpose in *new*IMAGES.

It was during INFORM 97 that we gave a party for the British trade mission to meet their counterparts, and to make our farewells. John Olsen kindly came, and spoke. Inevitably, the party was at Carrick Hill, a house outside Adelaide which was built in 1939 in the style of a late Elizabethan manor. Some of its windows, fireplaces and panelling, and a fine Jacobean staircase were brought from a Tudor manor house in England. The house was eventually given to the State, and is now available for hire for such occasions. It was particularly satisfying that two of the Clark brothers came. I had not seen them since soon after World War II when the Clark family left their house in England, just across the road from ours, to emigrate as '£10 Poms'. Hilary and I greatly enjoyed having a late dinner with these two clearly contented and now not so new Australians.

The UK has a two to one surplus in visible trade with Australia, and with most States and Territories. But not with South Australia, which has a healthy trade surplus with Britain. Much of that has to do with wine. The success of Australian wine exports to the UK is an impressive one: the initial invention of 'Chateau Collapseau' (the clever plastic foil inside a cardboard box and complete with tap); the marketing, including the leap upwards to medium-priced bottled wine; and the hygiene and quality of production—to name only a few elements of the success. ABCC winners to whom Premier Olsen presented the Awards at the lunch were the young, excellent Tatachilla Winery and Yummie Kitchen—who sell Christmas cakes to Brits! I tried hard but failed to recall the name of the British company which had then recently begun to sell rabbit fur to Australia for making hats—and that was before the calici virus was released!

I always enjoyed listening to both the South Australian premiers I knew, Dean Brown and John Olsen. Both had been notably kind hosts to visiting senior Brits, and it was also a pleasure to work with them directly and with their staffs. I was of course well aware of the political rivalries within the Liberal Party in South Australia, but I had good reason to understand and value the different but considerable strengths of both these political leaders. The UK has not only an unusual trading relationship with South Australia, but also a strong investment relationship. Just one example is the British Aerospace Australia offices and production facilities just north of Adelaide, and that company's acquisition of AWADI and its consequent position as a leading player in the Australian defence industry. All this, but primarily the opportunities for promoting trade, explains why, at a time of government financial restraint in the UK, we nonetheless managed to re-open a full-time British Consulate in Adelaide in 1995.

The ABCC lunch was also the occasion of our formal farewell to John Olsen. Naturally, I called on the Opposition too, and had a positive and lively talk with Deputy Opposition Leader Ralph Clarke about (along with other things) Indonesia, where I served before Australia, and on which my views were therefore often sought by Australians concerned with such a vital, complex—and impressively improving—relationship. Ralph Clarke is a man who, even in opposition, demonstrably enjoys his politics, I thought.

That evening, we drove to the warm welcoming Adelaide home of the helpful and admirable Heather and Peter (President of the Legislative Assembly) Dunn. We had been invited to dinner—a delightful, delicious informal dinner. We have much in common, including a deep admiration for Senator Margaret and Tom Reid. Peter and I also share a love of sailing. Peter had kindly arranged for me to be able to join the lovely vessel *One and All* for the Sydney–Hobart Race at the end of 1995, but our son Charles announced his dual intention, to bring his fiancée from the UK to Australia and to be married in our garden in Canberra—at the time of the race. My sound protestations that the last thing required at a wedding was the father of the groom were met, to my surprise, with adamant obstructionism and a hint of ridicule. I never managed to sail in a Sydney–Hobart, and it will remain one of my failed ambitions.

Peter Dunn is also a pilot, a farmer and a caring politician who has travelled enthusiastically and untiringly in South Australia, in the service of his electorate. Our conversation over dinner ranged from politics through sailing, farming and South Australians we knew to Westminster Speaker Betty Boothroyd. Altogether a very happy and memorable evening. I learned that Peter was to retire at the next election, to the evident regret of very many South Australians.

That evening was our last in Adelaide, we thought, but I was to return after RolleroundOz to try to help, with the lawyers concerned, in the wretchedly difficult and complex matter of the murder of the sister of a South Australian citizen in Saudi Arabia, allegedly by two British nurses. I was glad that before I left Australia an arrangement was reached which at least removed the threat of the death penalty.

Like so many other Australian State capitals, Adelaide had come to mean much to Hilary and me. The States differ so much from each other, and the personality of Adelaide and South Australia is unique. Many people think this is because South Australia was created by free settlers exclusively, but I am sure the character and quality of Adelaide is explained by more complex factors. There were the German refugees among the early settlers. There were the Cornish tin-miners. A Cornish Society exists to this day. I once opened an exhibition devoted to Cornish settlers in Adelaide, and learned much of their notable contribution to the development of South Australia. That said, I thought the Migration Museum in Adelaide was a touch coy and politically over-correct in its representation of immigrants and their relations with the Aborigines. Adelaide's Maritime Museum, which also covers immigration of course, is an excellent one, historically sound and rather inspiring. The Art Gallery of South Australia also excels as a rich museum and a modern gallery. Hilary and I from time to time would break away from an official programme for a dip into its treasures, following an introductory tour kindly given us by the Director.

Our memories of Adelaide also include the innovative design centre named for the former Jam Factory whose site it now occupies. Indeed, when our own system failed to find in the UK replacement blue glass inserts for the

Georgian silver salt cellars at Westminster House, the Jam Factory made some, perfectly.

But the most powerful and enduring memories of Adelaide for us are associated with the Adelaide Oval, and especially with Sir Donald Bradman. I took the then British Minister for Sport, Ian Sproat, to Rodney Marsh's Cricket School and to the Adelaide Oval. One of my staff had also taken him to Australian Institute of Sport establishments. Ian Sproat is an expert cricket enthusiast. He came at the time of the 1995–96 England Test Tour, when we fared so badly. As I saw it, the Minister came largely to help me share the shame! The best laid plans…Ian Sproat attended part of the first day of the only Test match England won in that series. By the time he returned to the House of Commons he could take full credit for this singular success.

But I was the more fortunate. On the second day of the match, Sir Donald Bradman came to watch. I met him and sat with him for a while, in fulfilment of every sensible boy's dream. He was then 86; was playing golf to his age; had an eye like a hawk; was wise, witty and still overqualified to be the inspiration he remains for his country. Discussing the physical exercises fielders were doing when they had a chance, presumably to develop reactions and stamina, qualities which The Don had had in abundance, I asked what sort of training he had done in England during those long tours when he had broken records and enthralled my country. With a twinkle he answered me in one crushing word: 'Batting!'. Although I never found the courage (or would it have been temerity?) to say that I recalled him being bowled for a duck by Eric Hollies in the 1948 Oval Test (which prevented a Test average of 100), I did wonder how many runs Sir Don thought he might score against this historically poor England side we were watching. He thought he might make about 65. Incredible. He could surely have done much better. His brilliant response to that view was: 'You have to remember I'm 86 years of age'.

Sir Donald did not bring his wife Jessie to the Oval. Jessie was ill, fighting her valiant and dignified fight against cancer. When she eventually died in 1997, I wrote to Sir Don. That there was a reply at all was impressive; that it was deeply moving was no surprise.

It was early in the same cricket match that Alexander Downer came to the Members' Stand for a short visit. He told me how he would be resigning the Liberal Opposition leadership the following day and becoming Shadow Foreign Minister. I admired his straightforwardness. He seemed to enjoy as much as we did a little incident after morning coffee when we returned to the Stand. He sat down to be greeted to his total surprise by the man sitting next to him—his former Radley Headmaster, by then Chairman of the MCC, Denis Silk.

Leaving the hotel for the drive north from Adelaide, we were photographed for the Adelaide *Advertiser* and some Sydney and London papers. A press photographer joined us in the Rolls for a score or so miles. Another worked from the windy back of a dual-cab ute. We stopped for more photographs at a petrol station. The Adelaide journalist had some amusing questions, including whether we had diplomatic immunity from the imposition of speeding fines. The answer was that in practice I would remove any diplomatic immunity of that sort British diplomats in Australia thought they might have; and we didn't speed, anyway. That said, I imagined the Rolls-Royce was looking forward to the open, non-speed limited roads of the Northern Territory.

We enjoyed the sight of Lake Bumbunga and its sandy shore decorated and enlivened by two close cousins of the Loch Ness monster. On closer inspection, they seemed likely to have been made from old truck tyre re-tread strips and scrap. It was here I did one of many radio interviews by telephone from the Rolls. It was hereabouts we learned much of the interesting development history of the region. There was the pipeline bringing water all the way from the Murray River to Port Augusta (and on to Whyalla) still running efficiently alongside the road. And it was hereabouts we first saw Stobie poles. These are telephone and electricity wire supports made of iron embedded in cement. The invention and its spread reflects the lack of tall trees in South Australia. Port Pirie has the world's largest lead smelter, we discovered. Just north of Port Pirie, we glimpsed the top of Spencer Gulf and the hills beyond, and to the right the dramatic Flinders Ranges began. On to Port Germein, which used to be a major seaport exporting wheat, with the longest wooden jetty in the southern hemisphere (5459 feet or 1664 metres!).

We had passed a trial crop-planting ground run by the impressive Commonwealth Scientific and Industrial Research Organisation, which itself is run by the redoubtable Sir Malcolm McIntosh. There has been a convention for many years under which members of Old Commonwealth countries may compete for some of the most senior civil service jobs in the others. That explained why Malcolm, an Australian, had for five years worked at Permanent Secretary level in Britain as Chief of Defence Procurement. He did a toweringly good job for the UK. It was by rather special coincidence that we had found ourselves in Buckingham Palace together one morning, being briefed most efficiently in the Green Room on how we were to be knighted by Her Majesty The Queen.

We were now in road train country, the beginning of a long but, I am glad to say, never excessively intimate association with these undisputed kings of the road. We passed through Stirling North and learned it was established in 1853 as the Minchin Well Camp for Aborigines. It later became a bullock-train camp which lasted until the railway between Port Augusta and Quorn was completed. Quorn, population 400, has a small garage selling BP petrol. At the back of it I found the man I should pay: he was deep inside the gearbox of a Model T Ford he was happily reconstructing. He gave me the usual good advice about the quality of the unsealed roads we were to take on our diversion from the simple straight route into the Flinders Ranges.

As we skirted Port Augusta that morning, we thought fondly of the Stuart Highway, the road leading north-west by Woomera and through Coober Pedy and on north to Alice Springs. We had visited the Alice a number of times by air, but the southern half of the Stuart Highway and the Red Centre by road we would have to miss.

Some 200 km north of Port Augusta we turned east at Parachilna to drive on a gravel road through five fords.

The Rolls took these with no change in its low murmur of contentment. The same was true of the dry stony river beds, though we drove slowly. We admired the old big red gum trees flourishing by the river beds and the old big red kangaroo chewing by the side of the road. We took, assuredly, some particularly fine photographs and video film, including of the Rolls crossing the fords.

Our object in making this diversion into the Flinders Ranges was to visit Blinman, which is Hilary's maiden name. We wondered whether there might be a family connection with one Peg-Leg Blinman, who discovered a modest amount of copper there in 1859—enough, just, for him to raise a family and, in Blinman's heyday in the 1870s, to support a population of 1500. There are now just a few pieces of old mine machinery and a very few old homesteads in and around Blinman. With Peter Dunn's and the South Australia Parliamentary Library's help, we discovered that Peg-Leg Blinman, shepherd before copper miner, had come from the same part of Somerset as had Hilary's father's family, so there was a link to explore. And from the sepia photograph of him and his family on the wall of the Blinman pub, we judged that Peg-Leg was quite a character, tough and humorous. He would have needed to be both.

The permanent population of Blinman now, we learned, is fifteen. From behind the bar we were warmly greeted by a voluble, cheerful lady who told us she was a bush-bunny. She noted 'that's a flash car', and asked for my business card for the pub wall. We were to find this method of decorating pub walls quite frequently in the outback: perhaps it's really a method of avoiding decorating! 'Bush-bunny' read aloud every word and letter on my card: title, Government crest, *new*IMAGES logo, and so on, and after a pause asked 'Whaddawe call you then Sunshine?'. I replied that 'Sunshine' would do just fine, thank you. 'Bush-bunny' served us the inevitable and delicious toasted sandwiches, and joined us for a chat. She was full of fun. We learned that she commuted to Blinman for a fortnight at a time, was a Girl Guide and Brownie leader, and knew and admired Dame Roma Mitchell. 'Bush-bunny' decided Murray could be called 'Sunshine' too. As we reluctantly took our leave, she gave Hilary a big hug. Outside, on the steps of the pub, Blinman's few men asked a string of knowledgeable technical questions about the Rolls-Royce. As we drove out of Blinman south through the Flinders Ranges, Hilary announced a subtitle for RolleroundOz: 'Two Sunshines and a Sheila'.

The colours of the Flinders Ranges in the late afternoon sun are glorious: reds, deep reds, golds, and many blues and greens. A wedge-tail at his food was hounded by a storm of crows and galahs. As the sun sank and we left the Ranges and rejoined a sealed road, we concluded again that the Silica colour of the Rolls (it used to be called Champagne Oyster) is just right for outback Australia. Nonetheless at Port Augusta, as every evening, Murray cleaned the car.

Port Augusta is aptly known as the crossroads of Australia. The direct rail connections with Perth, the Alice and Sydney made me wonder how Port Augusta will develop once the long awaited Adelaide–Darwin railway from the Alice to Darwin is eventually completed—as I now believe it will. Port Augusta's coal-fired power stations, for example, already supply over a third of South Australia's electricity.

The next stage was to drive both sides of the Eyre Peninsula and up to Ceduna. We crossed the bridge at the top of Spencer Gulf and looked down on the sun bouncing off yachts in deep blue water. Going on south from Port Augusta we reflected on the fact that saltbush fed lambs are sold as a speciality of the area through which we were driving. That struck us as a good way to make a marketing virtue out of a pastoral necessity: saltbush seemed the only food available. Once on the Eyre Peninsula, the farmland looked distinctly productive, the best we had seen in South Australia.

The scenery on the Peninsula is unexpectedly varying. For the first time we learned the Australian term 'jump-up' for the hills which appear to do just that from a flat landscape. Avenues of Stobie poles heralded the approach to Whyalla. At first sight, Whyalla looks rather sad: very much a steelworks town with concomitant pollution. Buildings are tinged brown. It is a far cry from Hummock Hill, as Captain Flinders first found and named it. But there were redeeming features including, for me, the return of a 650-ton World War II corvette to a resting place of honour in the city of her birth and of her name.

Franklin Harbour below Cowell caught our attention and imagination. The name was evidently given by Governor Gawler after the explorer and later Tasmanian Governor, Sir John Franklin, who, appropriately enough, had been a midshipman on Captain Flinders's ship *The Investigator*. It is a fine large harbour and the waters around evidently provide a rich and varied harvest of fish.

Cowell (named for yet another Pom) houses Australia's only commercial jade operation, exporting nephrite jade from the nearby Minbrie Ranges. Leaving Cowell, we realised we were quite close to Cleve and the Dunns' farm. The road was now straight and flat: silvery-green saltbush against golden sandy soil stretched as far as the eye could see in the morning sun.

We turned on the car radio and were pleasantly surprised to hear the King's College Choir from Cambridge singing *The Beatitudes* on FM.

Attractive Port Lincoln, almost at the foot of the Eyre Peninsula, was busy that Saturday morning and as the Rolls rather sedately approached a rare parking spot a local police car swiftly grabbed it ahead of us. The policeman flashed us an apologetic grin as we sought a parking spot farther away, just as a rain shower began and we had to walk back to a coffee shop. We enjoyed again wrought iron lace-work on some Port Lincoln houses and hotels. The early settlers clearly had a large range of fine harbours to choose from. What a long and interesting haul from the sailing ships of the 1800s to the container ships in Port Lincoln today.

We took a side-road to Coffin Bay. We stopped and walked, searching for Annie's Kitchen—famed for its oysters. We finally found the place, but we had selected the wrong season: Annie's was closed. We sought out the pub and the toasted sandwiches we knew must both be there, as everywhere.

Following the publicity our trip had already engendered, we should not have been surprised to have been recognised over our sandwiches and lemon, lime and

Australian Food

I think there is no cuisine unavailable in Sydney or Melbourne. Asian dishes are especially fine. Western cuisine in Australia is as sophisticated as anywhere. 'Aussie' staples include the 'pie floater'. A British Foreign Secretary, Douglas Hurd, once enjoyed this meat pie and gravy dish at a mobile wharfside café in Sydney. 'Bush' food covers a broad range of ingredients from traditional yet sophisticated Aboriginal herbs, grubs, roots, berries and shrubs of medicinal efficacy to emu, camel and crocodile. Interestingly prepared emu can be worth eating. Crocodile is not our favourite, but kangaroo fillet steak with a blackcurrant sauce was a much-applauded speciality of our English chef, Varena Hardy, at Westminster House, the British High Commissioner's official residence in Canberra.

bitters. An unlikely trio greeted us: a Harley-Davidson rider from Elliston, a Vietnam Vet on four wheels and a Coffin Bay worthy. We chatted animatedly, and were given a vivid and helpful account of road conditions in Western Australia by the Harley driver. The obligatory but, in his case, particularly high standard of leather dress and accoutrements made the Harley driver look like a rhinestone cowboy: he was a fine lunch companion and a fine South Australian. I told him of the previous British Consul-General in Sydney, Roy Reeve (now Ambassador in Kiev), who rode a Harley-Davidson—including to the office, followed by the official Jaguar carrying his briefcase. The Vietnam Vet was a well organised, thoughtful and philosophical fellow with soulful eyes and an easy manner. The man from Coffin Bay seemed satisfied but entirely unsurprised to have such a varied collection of visitors. Australians outside the main cities are pretty hard to surprise. The occasional roadhouse owner would tell us that in many years of running the place, he had not seen a Roller before, but he was stating a fact and expressing pleasure: had seen too much of life and of interest to be surprised at anything.

We drove north again through drier land, save for lovely Lake Hamilton. The coastal sand dunes seemed to shelter the onion weed by the side of the road and the early outings of butterflies. Elliston was notable for its murals—not only on the public toilets. They were well done. They were reflected later on Stobie poles in Waterloo Bay. Another short diversion took us to Venus Bay and its wind farm. A summer holiday centre, the permanent population of Venus Bay is fifteen. A caravan site proprietor came out of his house to wave us over for a talk about seasonal economic fluctuations, power for caravan sites and his family. And would we please pose with the Rolls in front of his caravan park sign? I hope we see the new brochure…

On north-west again through Streaky Bay, where a white-tie Masonic gathering was assembling. It was not yet five o'clock in the afternoon and I wondered why such an event was starting quite so early. Speculation on that engaged me while Hilary drove along this lovely coast, so different from the eastern side of the Peninsula, and into

Ceduna for dinner and an overnight stay. At the restaurant of a pleasant motel in Ceduna we ate fresh tasty barramundi accompanied by mountharries, which not even Murray had known before. They are reddish-green bush berries the size of blueberries and have a taste which reminded Hilary and me of an early Kentish russet apple. And so to bed, to think of the Nullarbor to come, but to dream happily of the Southern Ocean on one side of the Eyre Peninsula, of the Spencer Gulf on the other side, and of bush-bunnies in Blinman.

3 Across the Nullarbor

Day 7 would be 1228 km long. So we left Ceduna in the hour before dawn. The sky was full of those brilliant Australian stars. When seen from Australia, the Milky Way is so dense it merits being renamed the Creamy Way. But it is always a little startling to see Orion upside down, his dagger hanging upwards. Perhaps one should think of the dog-star Sirius as Orion's falcon. Later, the air seemed crammed with the pre-dawn birds' chorus. On balance, as the dawn broke over our right shoulders an hour later than Canberra, we thought it a good thing to have left thus early. The earliest pink-tinged light through the gum trees and the scrub was unusual: soft and beautiful. But it also began to illuminate, front of stage, bloody heaps of mangled animals along the road. In the half light, a road train travelling east flicked a stone at us. Good shot: our first—tiny and only—chip in the windscreen. And as we were to note gratefully throughout this trip, however long, large, heavy

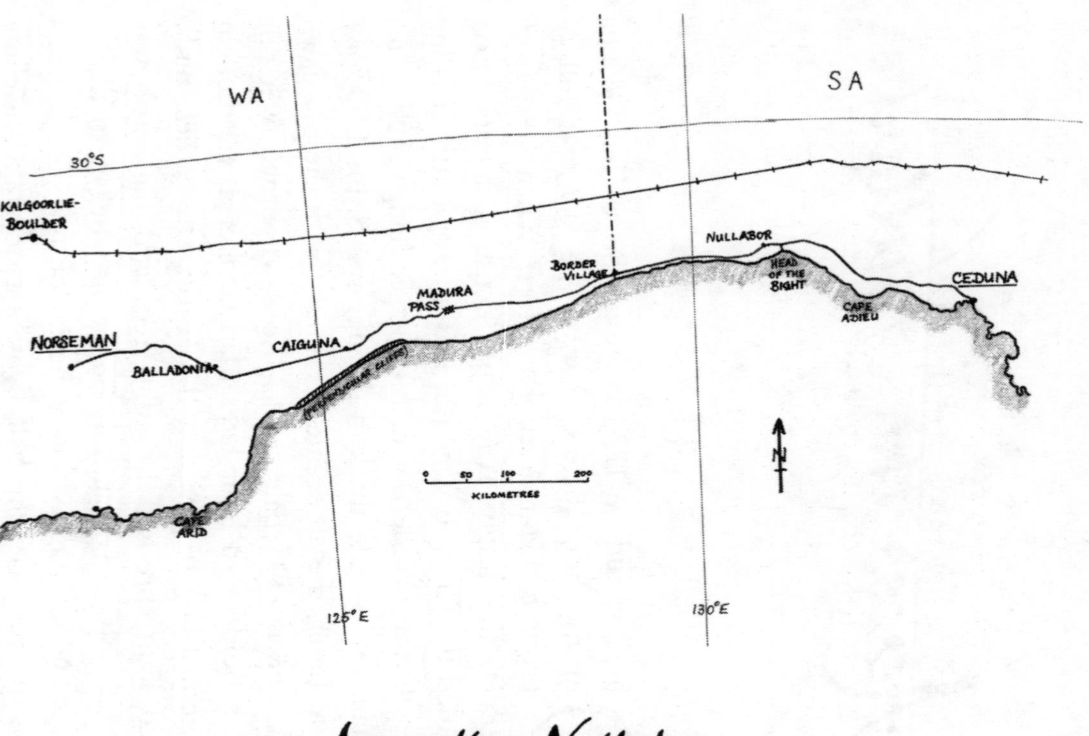

Across the Nullabor

and fast they were, road trains coming the other way rocked the Rolls not a jot.

The morning sun seemed to focus like a spotlight on an iridescent green, black and gold parrot: a first for us. But again the Aussie system of checks and balances operated: the sun also shone on a few dead cars abandoned in the scrub.

We heard Macca on the radio that Sunday morning. His show is a particularly effective mixture of radio devices. The phone-in part caused me to consider telephoning myself from the Nullarbor via the satellite telephone. That could have been a first for Macca. But the more we listened, the more I understood, with Murray's help, that this was a quintessentially Australian programme, for Australians at home and abroad. Any attempted intervention by me would have been an unwarranted, even rude, intrusion.

The sun was well up as the trees either side of us suddenly disappeared: nullus arbor. But the treeless part, nullus arbor per se, seemed short-lived. Indeed, despite what we had been told to expect, the Nullarbor, emphatically, is not boring. The variety of flora and fauna, the geology, weather (that day) and much else captivated us and provided food for much thought and consultation of guide books. This unexpected variety also inspired philosophic discussion, and even speculation between us as to whether we could ever fully understand Aboriginal painting. Driving as opposed to flying across the Nullarbor allowed us to see and ponder so many different scenes. Some, in their own variety of ways, recalled dot-painting, for example.

The Macca Phenomenon

The ABC broadcasts an extraordinary radio programme on Sunday mornings. Lasting 2 hours, it is hosted by a real pro, Ian McNamara, who, as is inevitable in Australia, is known as Macca. In a unique magazine format broadcast from Sydney and the provincial centres he visits, he plays music, and talks to Australians who live primarily outside the main centres of population and abroad. Homesick Australians telephone the programme from public phone boxes across the world, vying for time with outback dwellers. The formula includes stories about Australians of today, nostalgia, homespun philosophy and Australiana. It works exceptionally well, binding far-flung Aussies together and promoting a feeling of warm nationalism and friendly well-being. Macca is part of countless Australian family Sunday mornings.

While I think of Aborigines, I should confess that I had assumed without much, if any, thought that 'Nullarbor' was an Aboriginal name. I was a little comforted to find around Australia that I was not alone in this misunderstanding. Eventually I concluded that nullus arbor, added to the 90 mile straight at the end of the Nullarbor, was final proof of Roman occupation of Terra Australis—not quite so Incognita as Captain Cook was led to believe!

A rain shower produced a series of full bright rainbows against dark clouds. Murray was driving. Hilary lowered the front passenger window to take a picture-postcard of a photograph. The first draft of the valedictory despatch I was writing in the back seat flew around the car like giant confetti. After the rain, Hilary was at the wheel. Five brindle kangaroos came to the edges of the road, close together, to sip the accumulated water. Hilary slowed, switched on the hazard lights and used the middle of the road, carefully. The kangaroos eyed us all inquisitively and then hopped away, reluctantly and with the disappointment clear in their eyes, save for one brave, persistent and evidently thirsty male. A dingo crossed the road a little later with a mouth over-full of dead kangaroo. I wondered: if road trains are the lion-kings, are dingos the hyenas? There was really very little other traffic about: we felt rather privileged. We listened to CDs of Beethoven (real music, Klaus Zeller, my German ambassadorial colleague, would say), Vaughan Williams (real English music) and the Spinners (Liverpool folk music). The Spinners, singing a memorial to that evocative and much loved English artist Lowry, were poignant. Classical music on the Rolls-Royce hi-fi system suits this classic drive as well as the grand coastline of the Great Australian Bight close to and just south of the road for mile after mile.

We turned south and drove a few kilometres to that coast. We were at the Head of the Bight on top of the magnificent cliffs. We watched seven whales, including five mothers with calves, mostly close in to the cliffs, and a male further off. It was thrilling. The waves were very blue and the Great Southern White Whales almost beautiful in their lumbering, Leviathan, careless dominance of their natural environment, the sea. The mother whales seemed to be teaching their young to swim, and enjoying it. The male, distancing himself from childish play, might have been keeping watch, had it been possible to conceive of a threat to such monsters. Indeed, I supposed the whales knew they were safely away from even the shipping lanes. Further along the Bight, the deep blue sea was curling and breaking in massive explosions of spray on the now sun-drenched cliffs. How much better a view and an experience all this was than the sight of the same place from 30 000 feet up, our usual vantage point. And we had enjoyed that too, every time we flew that route. We chatted with other whale watchers. They were as impressed and awed as we were, including a couple who recognised us from the ABC's *7.30 Report*. As we walked back to the car, small busy birds chased around the cliff tops and warbled like larks. As we drove back to the main road, the road trains, now at right angles some 3 km away, looked as attractive and manoeuvrable as Dinky toys.

Beyond the Trans-Australia Railway, some 150 km to the north and east of us as we turned west on the main road again, was the Defence Reserve Restricted Area of Maralinga. This was the site of nuclear bomb experiments in the 1950s, run by the British and with Australian support. At the end of the experiments, an extensive clean-up exercise had been performed. But by the 1990s it had become clear that the technology of the 1950s could be significantly improved upon. Despite a signed agreement between the two countries in the 1950s expressing satisfaction at the clean-up, the two governments eventually agreed in 1994 to share the cost of another exercise, using state of the art technology. Britain agreed to contribute some $A40 million. Hilary and I had flown with Australian experts and a British government scientist on my staff to look over the area and report to London. This was a careful expedition, during which we learned a great deal.

In Maralinga, we learned something of the unique beauty of the real outback, of the glory of clear nights and stars seen with no light pollution. We saw Sturt peas for the first time—in the middle of the night as we drove to collect supplies from the Tea and Sugar train, which slowed and stopped at the flash of our headlights. We saw strong evidence of a clean-up as good as could have been done in the 1950s. We learned about modern techniques—for example, vitrification rather than just deep burial of contaminated materials. We learned that the background radiation at Maralinga village was several times lower than in a sandstone house in Sydney. We learned much more, including what splendid and devoted people the members of the Australian Protective Service are: those stalwart souls who look after the Woomera Prohibited Area, including Maralinga. (They produced a magnificent barbecued feast, at which they allowed BYO, but all wine drunk had to be red—a tradition unexplained, despite our enquiries. Perhaps it had to do with the red soil: spills would not show.) And we learned something about the Maralinga Tjarutja Aboriginal land and the Pitjantjatjara people. I was particularly pleased, later, to talk about it all with the then Chairman of the Aboriginal and Torres Strait Islands Commission, Lois O'Donoghue. And I was able to conclude that the British taxpayers' money would be justifiably and well spent.

We had lunch in Nullarbor Village, a small collection of a few buildings—petrol station and cabins grouped together to form a motel in the middle of nowhere. We requested the quickest snack and we were the only customers, but lunch came slowly, at the gentle pace of Nullarbor life. Later, we overtook a lone cyclist. We exchanged respectful salutes. Mad dogs, Englishmen and Aussie battling bicyclists…A wedge-tailed eagle stood atop a dead kangaroo at the road's edge as we approached. It stayed there, disdainfully, not a feather ruffled as we rushed by, cruise-control at the speed limit. We should have slowed, the better to see the eagle thus close; but I suppose that had we done so, he would have flown away: Murphy's Law of wedge-tailed eagles.

As the road parallels the long Great Bight coast just a few kilometres away, there are a number of turn-offs to view-points by the sea. These are essential, five-star stops. Although the traffic was very thin still, we did meet people at these view-points. They were retired couples brewing tea and proudly seeing their country at a distinctly slower and more intelligent pace than ours, and at an uncrowded, relatively fly-free and fresh time of the year. They were good people offering friendly chat and sound advice.

On west, we were still entranced by the so frequently changing vegetation. Thereabouts it was mostly small bushes, some flowering, some berried. The microwave links on tall masts and the thoughtfully provided water tanks which, for example, caravanners could use, were easier to see among the low vegetation. Another wedge-tailed eagle joined a crowd of crows at a kangaroo fest at the communal feeding trough, the road. Immediately, the wedge-tail established ascendancy and right of first selection from the menu.

We crossed the border into Western Australia. The vegetation continued to vary and delight. Taller bushes and denser scrub usually heralded the next scene of more trees, and two-tier gums I hadn't believed when I had seen them painted. We pulled off the road 100 m or so into a rest area to change drivers. The three of us wandered in three separate directions for a short walk. The bush was crawling, humming, buzzing, fluttering, glinting and glistening with life. It was also musical with bird song. The whole effect was lively and busy, yet calming after the road. Another sensible thing to do in a short break on the Nullarbor. We wished again that we could take more time on our tour around this lovely land.

Driving through Madura Pass was fascinating: we felt almost part of that geological shift as the rocks moved in on the road. The climb itself, and the descent were something of a shock after so many miles on the flat. We wondered why the name Madura? The guide books didn't help. To Hilary and me, until Day 7 of RolleroundOz Madura had meant that island of bull-racing off East Java, and the small collection we had bought of simple old Madura furniture. It was dark wood decorated with an eye for folklore and fun, mostly in golds and reds. One of the pieces is a small, handsome circumcision couch. The collection will surely one day enliven our guest bedroom in Tunbridge Wells!

We filled the tank with petrol at Caiguna. We had only two petrol stops in the 1228 km of the day. Murray had calculated that, with steady driving, the Rolls would do 600 km to a tank. The 90 mile straight begins near Caiguna. But the long road across the Nullarbor Plain has many far shorter but very straight stretches. Here and there on such straights, the road is marked to show that in time of need the Royal Flying Doctor Service aeroplanes use the road as an airstrip. They no doubt take care of people at the very occasional roadhouse and sheep station. Perhaps they deal with the unthinkable (and no doubt very rare) road accidents too. We were already fans of the Flying Doctors, and during RolleroundOz became keener fans than ever as we learned of the brave history and the complexity and ingenuity of this unique service to which such good people devote so much of their lives.

Something of a surprise: some large flat-bed trucks, heading east, were empty. But a greater surprise was the sole jarring sight of the day, towards evening: some 10 km of road-side litter near Balladonia. The sight recalled parts of western USA. Brown glass bottles are hardly biodegradable. Our spirits were restored by a cloud-spattered sunset before our destination for the day, Norseman.

We tried to avoid driving at dusk or later, including by setting off early. The drive across the Nullarbor was one of the very few days when dusk driving was inescapable. It is always harder work driving as the daylight declines, especially perhaps after being on the road all day. But touring in Australia presented the particular extra hazard presented by the practice kangaroos, wallabies and other wildlife—whether nocturnal by nature or not—have of moving from scrub or wooded land to the road at dusk. Their object is apparently to find water, or to graze by the side of the road. Even in some of the drier parts of Australia roadsides are often relatively well watered by rain, or even by dew draining off the road, or rain being sprayed on to the roadside by vehicles. And dusk is a favourite time, we found, for animals to begin to appear. The evidence before our eyes each morning demonstrated that the problem became significantly worse during the night, when so many more nocturnal animals are about. We wondered to what extent the various animals were attracted to vehicle headlights. One or two we met seemed mesmerised, rather like a family of badgers at play I met in a country lane in Kent one dark night. So that last hour driving into Norseman required extra concentration and care. I was glad to pull into the motel.

At the motel—for the first and only time throughout RolleroundOz—there was no hose available for Murray to wash the car, and it was particularly mud-spattered that day. The Rolls-Royce Silver Spur III is a very large car to have to wash down with numerous buckets of water from your motel room shower!

The motel had a good restaurant. Murray and I celebrated the crossing of the Nullarbor with steaks. Hilary failed to shame us as she simply savoured a Caesar's salad.

Crossing the Nullarbor in one day was a long drive; but it was never boring or banal. Nor was the Nullarbor barren. But one does have to look for life there, even in spring. We had a thoroughly interesting and happy day, and were captivated by the variety, the rarity and the specialised nature of so much we saw. We were alone for much of the time, and enjoyed that too, experiencing the evidence of the sparseness of the population of Australia away from the south-east and a few other main centres. We would like to cross the Nullarbor again, probably in the other direction to see things differently, and certainly at a slower pace. Two days would be five times better than one for this classic Australian experience.

4 Norseman to Perth

We passed a surprisingly and almost miserably cold night in Norseman. The motel time-switch ensured the heating was off until six o'clock in the morning, about the time we left. Clearly the freeze overnight was a surprise to the motel, and to Norseman too. The Rolls-Royce was covered in ice for the first time in its life. We were relieved but, as ever, unsurprised to find that the de-icing system worked very well.

Norseman had early gold finds and we made a detour to see the historic tailings. We learned that Norseman still attracts fossickers. We noted the post office—1896—and the statue of Norseman. This is not a Viking adrift, but a horse who pawed the ground, perhaps in impatience, but certainly helpfully since he thereby revealed gold. Norseman's cinema seemed to be a large steel shed. So did the Drop-in Youth Centre. Some small houses seemed to be made entirely of Colourbond steel, even the walls.

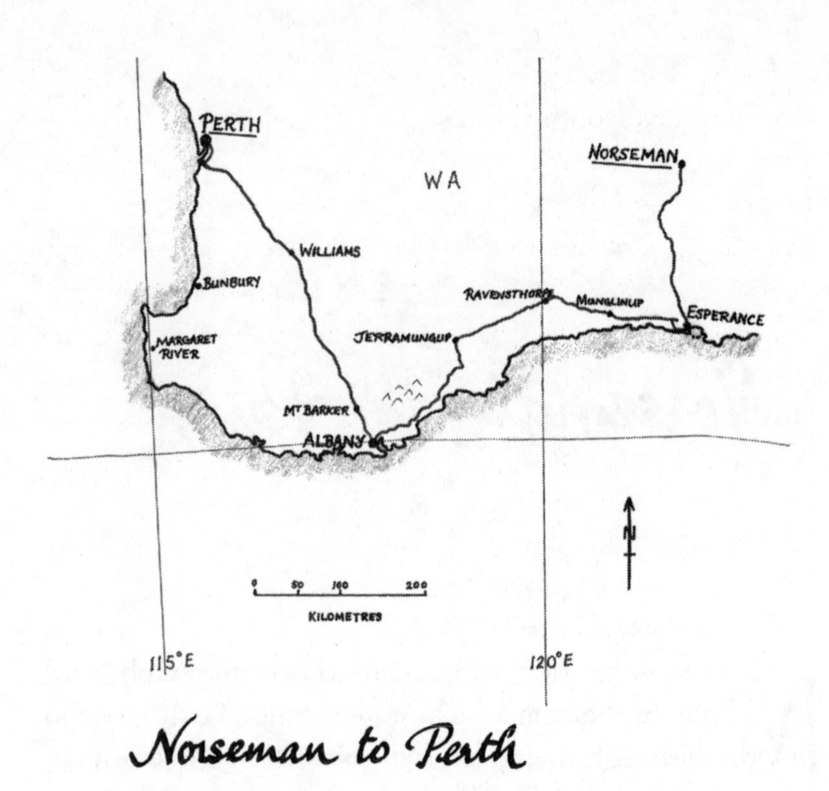

Norseman to Perth

We turned left, with an eye to the right on the northern road to Kalgoorlie, where a couple of years earlier we had had a day's intense learning about the gold industry, the super-pit and Kalgoorlie history. We had had dinner with one of Kalgoorlie's—and Western Australia's—greats of business, Geoff Stokes, who had recently died, very young, of cancer. A tragic loss of a man with much more still to give to his family and his country.

As we drove south, the morning shone like Norseman's early gold. So did Lake Dundas, Lake Gilmore and others as they reflected the gum trees through early sunlit mist. The frost glistened on the scrub. There were little clumps of lovely salmon gums, and a hamlet named after them. We continued south through grain country complete with silos and railway, and through Grass Patch, a railway halt named apparently prosaically, but charmingly. There were now broom bushes to be seen, and the occasional early yellow wildflower which we failed to identify from the wildflower books we carried. Further south we saw young green wheat and wattles. Later, waratahs, xanthorrheas and banksias abounded, and another unknown—a spiky bush with small open coral flowers. The reference books we had evidently confined their scope to the west of Western Australia. A school bus finally persuaded us that we did not have the road from Norseman entirely to ourselves. We watched the hedgerows reflected in water in the ditches alongside. The ice had now melted. We passed salt ponds and huge fields, some with oilseed rape in flower—although the crop did not look as lush as that we knew in Kent, subsidised by the Common Agricultural Policy.

I thought again, as I had so often in Australia, spurred by farming interests here and by long Australian memories of negotiations when the UK joined the then Common Market, that at last the imperative of European Union enlargement to the East might be the catalyst required for radical, as opposed to piecemeal and inadequate, reform of the CAP. I hoped; Britain hoped that our fellow EU members who resisted CAP reform would not seek to use the unaffordability of the CAP in an enlarged EU to attempt delay or to barter the terms of enlargement.

The route south was shared with the railway, whose principal purpose had to be the transport of wheat and other produce to the port of Esperance. We passed through Gibson Soak. I hoped that this place had not been named after a pond of some sort, but rather after a man it could have been fun to know. Further south, there was a subtle but insistent change in the landscape. Now influenced by the ocean, it was softer. There were sheep and cattle. The trees were larger. As we drove by someone in the woods was bagging strings of eucalyptus bark. The countryside was now increasingly manicured. A rise in the road gave us a view of Esperance's wind farm, but that morning there was no wind. Later, there was a fine view of the port of Esperance and the islands.

As we approached the town, dealers in agricultural machinery and motor cars lined the route flying their flags and bunting. *Esperance* was an excellent name for the French exploration ship which anchored here in 1792, and for which the town was named. But my disinterested observer status fell away again as I reflected proudly on Captain Cook, Matthew Flinders and so many other British contributors to Australia's development. We discussed explorers galore, and the financiers (whence else the backing for Australia's goldmines than London?). We used the word 'colonists' unashamedly, for the Australian colonies were notable successes; and, importantly, British governments of the times encouraged independence for many years before it came.

From earlier visits, Hilary and I had discovered that Esperance is a secret to most Australians. The town is the key to some of the world's best beaches and loveliest coastline. We had been privileged to drive a great deal of it in a four-wheel drive vehicle on our previous visit, and had marvelled at the tropical turquoise waters in the bays, at the miles of silvery virginal sand, and at a wallaby who was so chummy he almost petted us.

We toured around to show off the port and the town to Murray. We drove again along the scenic coastal drive. It did not disappoint us, and it thrilled Murray. The drive allows spectacular views including, that morning, curling theatre curtains of waves and theatrical effects of spray leaping into the air. We saw again the lovely islands off Esperance around which the early explorers had navigated so carefully, and recalled with pleasure that one of the islands was inexplicably called Charlie, the name our younger son has adopted as a modification from the correct but conventional Charles. We recalled too the hospitable and helpful Chamber of Commerce officials and other good people who had earlier shown us the coast, the port and the impressive development plans. And we remembered fondly the tour of Esperance Bay in a proud brand new tug. As we looked across at the islands, a whale-watching boat set off to sail among them, no doubt looking for whale cows and calves: this coast provides a number of favourite birthing places, as we knew, again from our earlier visit, when we had been entranced by the sight of a mother whale and a very young calf only yards from the shore.

We could stay no longer. We drove out past Pink Lake, so called because of the mixture of algae and salt which at some times of the year turns the whole lake a rose pink. Today there were only patches of pink, but the lake reflected the clouds prettily enough. We drove past the salt works and their young mountains of salt, and away from Esperance.

As we made progress towards Munglinup and Ravensthorpe, two big black Angus bulls sat statuesquely staring at each other in a small bright green paddock. High sand dunes appeared away to the left. A cheerful Canadian girl served us a bar lunch at Jerramungup. She was very much in charge of the hotel. The casual Australians around did her bidding unquestioningly. She was also very much in charge of her life. This should not have surprised us. The Australian Consul in Bali told us that in his experience Canadian travellers were the best organised of all. This one was an enthusiast for Esperance and its coastline, but she was working and holidaying her way around Australia and thinking of tearing herself away for the skyscrapers and sophistication of Melbourne. We offered her small portions of advice, and drove on towards Albany.

The striking Stirling Range appeared. The countryside was rich with sheep, cattle, yakkas with tall spikes, marsh reeds, horses, black cockatoos, wagtails, native flower cultivation and pockets of gnarled dead white gums, stark against green grass and blue sky. There was oilseed rape and much wheat. There were co-operative grain storage sheds, here called bins. There were some early wildflowers too, in vibrant, vivid colours. There were graceful feathery grasses. This was early spring in southern Western Australia. And it was complete with a station called Canberra West!

It was good to see handsome Albany and King George Sound again. As we drove to the hotel we passed Dog Rock. The dog was accommodating a seagull sitting on his nose. We had a fun dinner at Pyrmont House with friends from an earlier visit, Mayor Annette and Tom Knight, and the Jorgensens. The conversation included news of still further improvements to Albany, and of current problems. Having seen the drive and effectiveness of Annette's unpaid mayoral terms thus far, we had no doubt she would triumph again.

Next morning, looking out across the sea, we watched the sun rise. I did telephone radio interviews for the ABC and an Adelaide station. The fax was busy to and from Canberra. This was our first real hotel since Adelaide, and we had a pleasant suite. The image was amusingly marred for us by our washing and ironing in the suite. We planned and pursued our own tourist drive to show Murray the town, the Peninsula and the islands. In the morning sun, the old whaling station and quarantine hospital were particularly easy to pick out. So, too, was a fairly recent wreck. It had been a restaurant boat which, if I recall aright, had run aground while being moved. The US Navy had tried to refloat and shift her as a service to Albany, but the practical problems were too great. I had asked my Naval Adviser to see if the Royal Navy could do better, but his researches, sadly but inevitably, had led to the same conclusion. Nonetheless I was glad that HMS *Gloucester* had included Albany among her sixteen port visits around Australia that year. So, according to Annette, was Albany.

We had decided to drive to Perth direct by way of the Albany Highway, rather than around the corner via Margaret River and Bunbury. We were of course pressed for time; we had visited the south-west corner twice before (once on holiday from Indonesia); and the Albany Highway was new to us.

That said, the south-west corner of Western Australia will always mean much to us. It is full of amusing, kind and interesting people. Dr Jim Leavesley is one. In conversation with him we discovered that he had been a National Service doctor at RAF Padgate when Hilary's RAF officer father was posted there. Jim was later a hospital doctor in Perth, and the ABC radio doctor. Now retired from medicine, he is an author, philosopher, wit and gentleman resident of Margaret River. He and his wife once assembled a collection of brightly interesting people for coffee with us and the Consul-General in his garden. We learned so much from Jim and his friends. Then there was the winner of a viticulture gold medal for his wine, one of the most determinedly happy people I have met. He was also generous in his praise of others' wines—not, I was sure, just because of magnanimity in victory. Margaret River has a goodly number of rather small vineyards (British English for 'winery'), owned by retired professionals. The social effect of this influx of intellectual bright sparks upon a unique and lovely part of the world is almost tangible. Yet some vineyards there may be too small to make long-term economic sense. Mergers of some sort may have to come later.

The then Consul-General in Perth (now Governor of Montserrat), Tony Abbott, his wife Margaret and we had lunch one memorable day at the home of Bill and Pam McKay of Abbey Vale Vineyard. Bill is a lively, inventive polymath: expertise in viticulture is but one of his many strengths. I treasure the memory of our walk in the coastal

National Park near his home and our conversation about everything from the chemicals in the ground water, local planning and psychology, to the future of the Western world—all inspired by an amalgam of the coastal scenery and Bill's lateral thinking.

We were visiting the McKays in 1996 when that dreadful disaster happened at Yallingup: children and adults, sheltering from the rain under a cliff on the beach, were killed when the cliff fell on them. We sent condolences to Premier Richard Court, thought hard but had to decide we could do no good. Mixed memories, then, of the Margaret River region.

This was a pleasant drive through countryside which sometimes recalled parts of southern England. The growth of wine production east of the Margaret River in WA was illustrated within the first hour or so of the drive (and parts of southern England do produce wine, including the excellent white Chiddingstone, a wine we served proudly and to much acclaim in Canberra). The tallest unsupported television mast in the southern hemisphere (168 m tall, the guide book says) was a surprising sight atop Mt Barker. Throughout this drive, there were just occasional splashes of wildflowers. We also spotted a field with clumps of spinifex, which looked curiously like the old-fashioned stooks of wheat or barley which have not been seen for years, and which were replaced by those slices of giant straw Swiss roll, nowadays even wrapped in coloured polythene.

There was some very English-looking countryside at Williams—with a picturesque little river and weir. And we enjoyed the occasional patch of vivid blue leschenaultia which, we recalled, was a particular favourite of Margaret Abbott. The trunks of some spindly fir trees had been blackened by fire, but back-lit by the sun, they and the silvery sheen of the leaves would have inspired a theatre set designer. We saw orange and lemon trees heavily fruited, and a coral tree which seemed to be on fire, so bright were the flowers. Day 9 of RolleroundOz, 19 August (grandson James's birthday), it seemed early for spring, but spring had surely begun even as far south as southern WA.

We lunched on fish in Fremantle, overlooking the Indian Ocean. From the Tasman Sea via the Bass Strait, the Great Australian Bight and the Southern Ocean to the Indian Ocean, by Rolls-Royce! The Timor, Arafura and Coral Seas and the Pacific Ocean were to come. Meanwhile we looked across the water to Rottnest, and recalled the time we had visited the island for half a day, much assisted by a young Mauritian-Australian in the tourism office. When I told my Mauritian colleague in Canberra of her, he became understandably keen to visit Rottnest too. Rottnest, named for the quokkas—the abundant and friendly little marsupials mistaken for rats by an early Dutch navigator—is an attractive island indeed. Dr Bruce Arthur found that, too, after sailing his yacht with his wife Jane from their home in Queensland around the top of Australia, via a diversion, the Darwin–Ambon yacht race, and despite a nasty bout of Ross River fever. Bruce, also an ex-British doctor, from Norfolk, intended to SailaroundOz, but he and Jane were understandably seduced by Rottnest. They sold the yacht and stayed there for six months, Bruce working as a much liked locum. We had met these two splendid Australians first in Indonesia, where Bruce was the Australian Embassy doctor who also looked after Brits (the UK provides reciprocal services—for example, in New Delhi).

Fremantle was a favourite harbour of ours. We had first seen it on holiday, and had watched the replica of Captain Cook's *Endeavour* being built. We could not then have imagined that one day we would know the admirable Sir Arthur Weller, the man who inspired and led the Endeavour Foundation which he created after Alan Bond's financial collapse, and who did so much to make this the most accurate and precise full-scale ship replica ever built. Nor could we have imagined that we would sail in the *Endeavour* from Pittwater to the Sydney Harbour Heads and up to the Opera House the day she first arrived at her home port of Sydney.

We had last seen Fremantle the previous month, along with a UK Task Group of nine Royal Navy vessels led by an aircraft carrier with Admiral embarked, and including two nuclear submarines. The Task Group did many exercises with all three Australian Armed Services. Sea Harriers flew off HMS *Illustrious* near Bali, bound for RAAF Pierce, near Perth. They were refuelled in mid-air by RAF tankers. After landing at Pierce, they conducted state of the art exercises with the RAAF. There is a nice story of a standard answer the American Air Force is said to give to telephoned complaints about sonic booms: 'Sorry, ma'am; that's the price of freedom.' There were some complaints about sonic booms during these WA exercises, to which the RN's reply was: 'Sorry; but that's your chaps running away from ours.' That was a little rich,

I thought, even though RN Sea Harriers are subsonic and it was certainly the RAAF who had produced the sonic booms.

Altogether, the UK Task Group's visit was a particularly happy and successful one. Some senior Australians were good enough to fly across from the east for it. Notable among these was the Hon. Bronwyn Bishop, Minister for Defence, Science, Equipment and Personnel. She spent a good deal of time inspecting RN equipment. Bronwyn also came to the traditional cocktail party—for some 400 people—in HMS *Illustrious*'s huge hangar. Those present were treated to a Sunset Ceremony and display by the Royal Marines Band. The Band had played also at the then recent hand-over ceremonies in Hong Kong. On board *Illustrious*, playing superbly, they entered and left the hangar on the moving flat bed of the aircraft lift. They counter-marched the length of the hangar, while making memorable martial music. During the Sunset Ceremony, the Band played 'Advance Australia Fair' in an excellent arrangement. The Minister asked for a taped copy.

Admiral Alan West, in charge of the Task Group, had decided to have Admiral's Divisions, a formal parade, on the quayside at Fremantle. Thirty per cent of the ships' companies—some 750 men and women—were on parade. Alan West kindly invited me to join him at Divisions. As the parade marched past us, and as I walked round inspecting my allocated hundreds of smartly turned out men and women, with my Defence Adviser, Commodore Peter Wykeham-Martin RN in tow, resplendent in gold braid, 'scrambled eggs' and aiguillettes, there was a delectable irony. It was not so much in the smartness of the

Divisions measured against the reluctance of sailors to parade at all, and especially of submariners who had been at sea for months and had had to send home for dress uniforms. It was rather that when I had last had anything to do with Admiral's Divisions, it was during my National Service, 40 years earlier, and I was among the most junior sailors on parade. However, it was a serious privilege and an enormous pleasure to inspect, meet and talk with these fine representatives of the modern Royal Navy visiting a country with whom we had such deep, modern and confidential relations, and who had demonstrated so well the effectiveness and usefulness of those relations.

We drove into Perth after lunch for some work with the Consul-General Mike Horne, and to stay with him and Debbie. Hilary and I replied to fourteen welcome letters from schoolchildren and their teacher in Canberra. The children had written to us to establish contact, and in some cases to seek advice about a desk project of a theoretical drive around Australia they were researching. Several of them were particularly concerned about budget management. We were much struck by the generosity of their budget—several times our own! The Hornes kindly gave a relaxed and very pleasant buffet dinner party to allow us to say goodbye to the Consulate-General staff (and husbands and wives).

The next day was largely devoted to farewell calls. Mike Horne and I called on Premier Richard Court. The first few minutes were complete with television crew. I had always enjoyed conversations with Richard Court. This time we had a good economic and commercial discussion, and one on tax theory and practice, State and

Federal—a topical subject. It was instructive to hear the Western Australian view of the tax reform debate. The Premier was keen to establish, argue and pursue WA (and other State) advantage now that tax reform had been put on the national agenda by the Federal government. The history of State/Federal action and debate in the tax field is a fascinating one, with interesting constitutional implications. The right to levy income tax had been ceded in war time from the States to the Commonwealth, for sound national reasons. Although the States would like to have more revenue-raising ability, rather than to have to negotiate subventions from Canberra, I don't suppose they would relish the political incubus of once again being the income tax collector.

The Premier and I discussed *new*IMAGES, of which he spoke highly. We spoke too of the largest British trade mission ever to visit Australia as part of *new*IMAGES. The mission was some 100 strong, and devoted to the oil and gas industries. It had done many million pounds of business in the week or so it was in WA; and much more still was to follow. In my view, the inception, organisation and management of such missions by today's British Diplomatic Service and the Department of Trade and Industry is well done, effective and important.

Hilary joined us to call on Western Australia Governor Michael Jeffreys and his wife Marlena, who have done so much as stewards of Government House, and whom we much like and admire. At the end of the call, they showed us the latest refurbishments. We were to see them again that evening at His Majesty's Theatre. Other calls included the cheerful, forward-thinking Geoff Gallop,

The Commonwealth

The word Commonwealth has at least two meanings in Australia. The Commonwealth of Australia is the country's constitutional title. Commonwealth connotes, then, the entirety of the country, the sum of its State and Federal systems, and overall governance. Commonwealth also refers to the Commonwealth of Nations, which has a lower profile than it merits in Australia—in part because of the dual meaning. But Australia is an important member of and contributor in many ways to the Commonwealth, of which HM The Queen is head, and there are a number of active societies—in Canberra and the State capitals—devoted to the support and pursuit of Commonwealth aims and principles of cooperation and assistance among the 50-plus members around the world.

Leader of the Opposition in WA, and a friend from Oxford of Tony Blair's. It was good also to say farewell properly to the Lord Mayor, Dr Peter Natrass, a recent kindly and thoughtful host to his opposite number from London; and to friendly Speaker Hon. George Strickland, whom I had earlier met on board HMS *Illustrious*. We could not see his predecessor, Jim Clarko, who had been so hospitable (for example, to visiting British Members of Parliament), nor former President of the Legislative Assembly Clive Griffiths. Jim had retired and Clive had been appointed Western Australia's Agent-General in London.

Mike Horne had organised both an instructive and pleasant lunch with some business leaders, and a large official farewell cocktail reception at the Parmelia Hilton where Hilary and I had so much and so often enjoyed staying. Ruth Harrison, Rolls-Royce owner, runs the hotel so well, and with such a civilised touch. At the cocktail party, the Hon. Mike Board MLA represented the Premier, and spoke kindly and well. Mike Board made clear that it was his view also that *new*IMAGES was going well in Western Australia. The reception allowed us to say goodbye and thanks to so many people, including the present and past Commodores of the Royal Perth Yacht Club, Bob Trotter and John Flower. They had been extraordinarily good hosts at the Yacht Club, whose endeavours we admired and whose atmosphere we loved. And John Flower had handed me the helm of his fast and thrilling racing yacht! Professor Don Watts kindly came too. We had met first in Darwin in 1994 at the technology park he was then running. We had kept in touch. He and Michelle had entertained us in Perth. Don had given me useful learned papers. I had given him less. We had often met each other on aeroplanes, and promptly abandoned the work we had with us in favour of good conversation over a glass of Ansett's wine.

Somehow, amidst driving us to all these engagements, Murray had also managed to squeeze in a light service for the Rolls at the helpful Chellingworth Motors. It was not a surprise that no problems were found, as Murray reported when he drove us to His Majesty's Theatre to join the Governor's party for *La Traviata*, a favourite opera of ours. Our liking for it may have been sharpened by our attendance at the National Opera House in Bulgaria in 1963 when two British singers sang the leads in *Traviata* in an international competition. Alberto Remedios was the tenor, but was really Albert Reems, if I recall aright, former centre-half for Brighton's soccer team. He sang with strength, accuracy and verve in support of Ava June Cooper as Violetta. Ava June won the competition to great acclaim. *La Traviata* in Perth was a first class production with superb sets, more than matched by the intelligent and masterly singing of the role of Violetta. Verdi, *La Traviata* and the Australian National Opera thus provided the finale to a most pleasant and memorable day of farewells to Perth.

5 Perth to Broome

Verdi was still ringing in our ears as we left the Consul-General's Residence in Dalkeith next morning, Day 11 of RolleroundOz. Ann Douthwaite, my Personal Assistant, had by now joined us. A television crew from *A Current Affair* filmed our fond farewell of the Hornes and of Perth. As we drove with the morning traffic through Perth, the crew's car kept pace with us in the next lane to the right. It was a surprise to see the cameraman open the passenger door and kneel in front of the seat to film with the camera held outside, close to the ground. This ensured a fine shot, with Perth's elegant modern steel and glass skyscrapers forming a handsome background to the Rolls-Royce. Hilary filmed the crew filming us, but she worked from an open window, not an open door. Again she took some good video. We were to see the Perth crew for *A Current Affair* again, much further north, and we were much to enjoy their company.

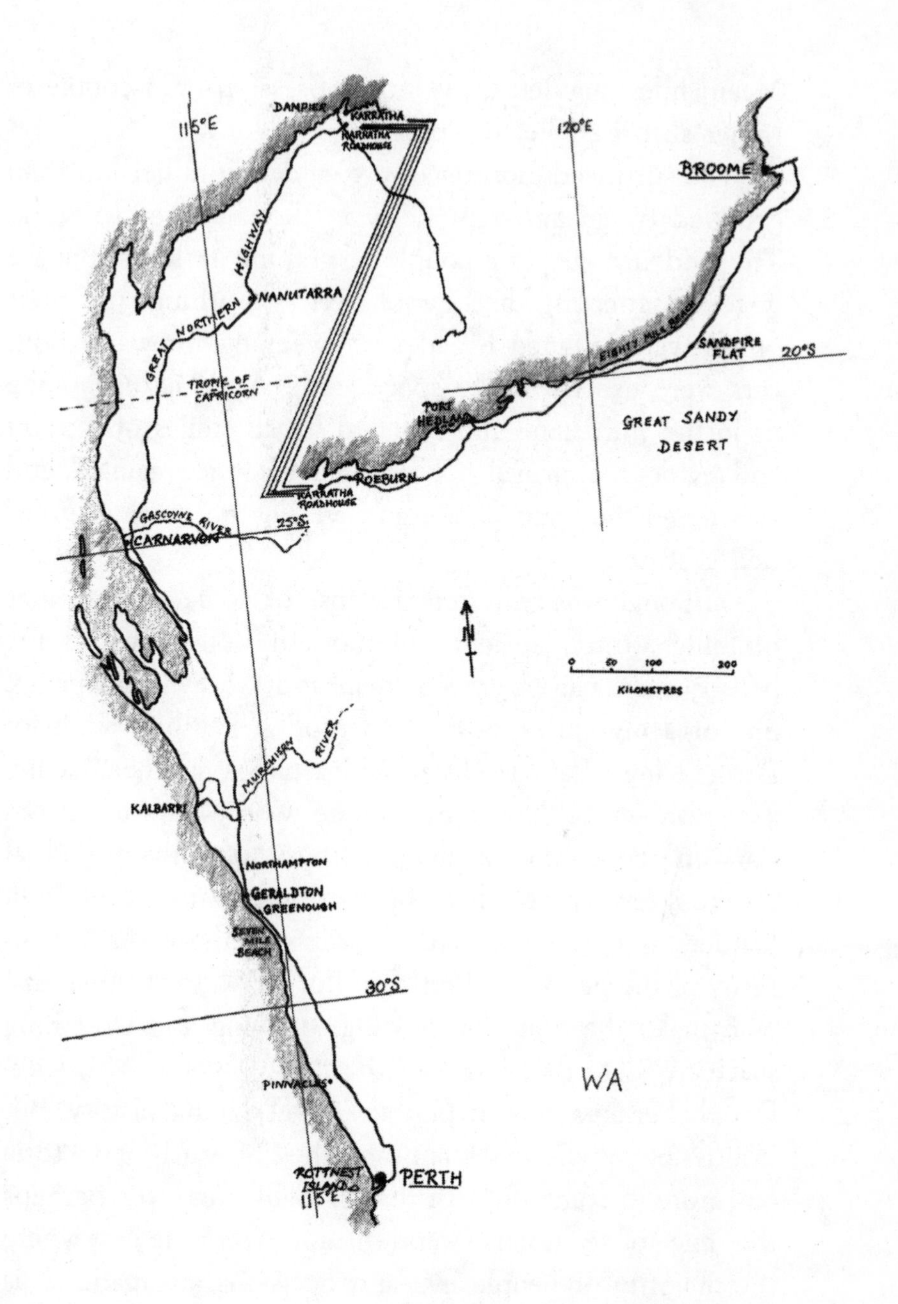

Perth to Broome

Meanwhile, they left a distinct impression on a couple of rather surprised Perth motorists.

The surprised motorists were evidently rather less than gruntled by an apparent delay in their journey to work. The evidence was in a couple of graphic gestures. But we were not affecting the flow of Perth's morning rush hour on its well-designed broad and sweeping freeways. Both cars were exactly at the speed limit. A police car joined us in the third lane and radiated broad smiles of interest and evident approval. The police presence calmed and sweetened the atmosphere, and we saw no more disgruntled gestures.

Although we regretted the loss of some of the older buildings, those elegant tall modern buildings and the broad greensward between them and the Swan River are one of a myriad of positive memories we shall retain of Perth. King's Park in differing seasons is another. Laying a wreath on 11 November at the War Memorial in the Park in the company, among others, of former Federal Senate President Michael Beahan and Army Chief John Sanderson is a particularly moving memory. As are so many of the people of Perth, and of all Western Australia, who make the State an exciting, growing and refreshing place. A State that has something in common with California. Perhaps it is in part the gold mining history. But it must be much more than that: the gold rush of Victoria has more in common with that of California. It is perhaps the sense of separateness and distance from the east where the majority of people live and decisions are made. It is easy to find both Californians and Western Australians who at least affect to ignore the Federal capital, and in many cases probably do just that. At all events, there is in Western Australia a sense of something approaching independence and certainly a sense of independence of spirit, allied to the spirit of pioneering.

I think it not too far-fetched to suggest that there is even something of this spirit in the financial world of Western Australia, probably because it is so close to and supportive of not only the mining industry, but also of the bold, exciting world of the North-West Shelf and its ventures. I felt this on my first official visit to Perth when Chris Wiggins, Director of Rothschild Australia Ltd, was host at a lunch with the mining and energy community. There I first met Bill Gash, then the Energy Minister, who seemed much imbued with this spirit as well as with considerable expertise. And we found that spirit in spades in Alan Birchmore of Chalfont Management and his wife Jill. The Birchmores were generous hosts and flew us to Kalgoorlie and Meekatharra a year or so into our posting in Australia. They did so for our necessary education, and in the most enjoyable way. It surprised only us that Jill flew in a light aeroplane and clambered about mines with one leg encased in plaster, wielding crutches.

We turned north to join the Brand Highway, and thus to begin the long west coast stretch. Over to the west, we caught a glimpse of the Pinnacles, those eerie and spiky fossils: it is hard to believe they are the remains of an aeons-old forest. We slowed and pulled over as we met an escort vehicle leading a large portable house in three sections carried by three flat-bed trailers. Beyond, when the dust settled, we could see a few wildflowers beginning to show (it was 21 August). We noticed some striking banksias and, with the morning sun behind it, a delicate white shrub which evidently, and justly, is known here as smoke-bush.

The Brand Highway makes its way in two steps to run alongside the Indian Ocean at Seven Mile Beach. Just north is Greenough, where trees are bent like angle-irons from the salt in the ocean winds—a curious effect. We had an excellent fresh fish and salad lunch at the Greenough Resort, where we stayed overnight. The proprietor photographed the Rolls, evidently a first at his welcoming resort. While I did an afternoon's work, the resident St Bernard insisted on accompanying Hilary as she set off to walk 5 km by the river, across a sandbar and along the dunes, enjoying also wildflowers and blue Indian Ocean waves, and pondering the stories of the many wrecks along this coast. The St Bernard gave up after a kilometre and a climb to the view-point he obviously favoured too. A delightful and memorable dinner among Poms and Aussies also enabled us to learn about Geraldton, through which we drove next morning.

Geraldton's primary importance is as a port and commercial centre exporting grain and mineral sands. As in so many distant parts of Australia, children on the outskirts of Geraldton rise early and wait by the road for their school buses. It was a bright sunny morning, but a little chilly, and the children were warmly dressed. The car radio told us that the temperature that day in Broome would rise to 30°C. No doubt the temperature would rise a little in Geraldton also, enough to help the tomatoes grow. Tomatoes grow all year round in Geraldton, and keep the many honesty boxes (buckets or boxes serving as unmanned tills) outside houses filled. The price that day for 2 kg was $1.00!

This was a morning for powerful blues, notably that of the Indian Ocean and of fields full of Paterson's Curse. Murray had told us three years before how this striking mauve-blue weed is known as Paterson's Curse because it chokes out good grass. At least that is the case in normal years. In times of drought, the name changes to Salvation Jane, because the weed will grow when grass will not, and it does contain some nourishment for the stock. We wondered whether in this year of El Nino the more flattering name would need to be used.

On north through pretty Northampton with its picturesque old railway station. The population is now 780. The town was founded in the 1830s to exploit the local lead and copper, and as a centre for hiring convicts. We found it intriguing that Western Australia's first public railway should have run from Geraldton to Northampton, rather than in the Swan River region. Beyond the town, there were now countless wildflowers as well as blue and white fields of cultivated lupins. The wildflowers decided us on a diversion to Kalbarri through its National Park to the sea. As we drove through the National Park, the Rolls and we were flanked magnificently for miles by an extraordinary array of wattle, wild flowering shrubs and wildflowers, all in brilliant bloom. This was better than the tales we had heard, better than the books we had read. How Agnes Fisher back at Westminster House in Canberra—who understood and arranged flowers so well—would have appreciated this abundance, this profusion of dazzling floral diversity! We stopped to look more closely among the pink and white carpets of wildflowers. There Murray found a shiny brown beetle who seemed to have mistaken a shiny brown beer bottle for a mate. Curiously enough, a radio show compere had told me during a broadcast of this happening on the Nullarbor. We wondered whether the beetles were related. This bottle was quite well-hidden and we saw no others, unlike on that stretch of road near Balladonia as we crossed the Nullarbor. Ah well…as long as the bottles don't mate.

Back on the main road north, National Route 1, and at a petrol stop, Ann spotted an army vehicle based on a Land-Rover. From her discussions with the driver, she learned that it was a mobile workshop, returning to Perth from a paratroop training exercise at RAAF Exmouth. A police car preceding a very oversized load of mining equipment made it clear we should move right off the road. We obeyed, and were grateful for the advice and glad we had followed it. So, we imagined, were the two tankers stopped ahead of us, despite the amount of rubber they had left on the road as they braked. The smell of the burned rubber and the thunder of the hard-pressed loaders carrying the mining equipment disturbed a crow sitting on a nest in a roadside tree. There were several other nests nearby. Noisy accommodation, but location is all, and these nests were right next-door to that community canteen for carnivores, the road.

We stayed the night in Carnarvon, a town of banana plantations, of ruby grapefruit, bright star fruit and vibrant bougainvillea of all colours. We were struck by the unusually wide streets and learned that this was because 100 years ago goods were transported to and

Australian Birds

An American wag once said there were only four kinds of birds: pigeons, seagulls, small brown birds and others. Australia has all four, but especially others: a remarkable and colourful collection of birds, a few introduced but mostly native. There is an interesting avian–human correlation noticeable in maps of distribution of Australian birds and population. In the remoter parts we found extraordinary birds such as wedged-tailed eagles, and oval clouds of budgerigars. Our garden in Canberra was rich with parrots of all kinds. We were especially fond of the lorikeets and crimson rosellas; less so of the battalions of sulphur-crested cockatoos, which destroyed our tennis net and artificial turf. But we thought the kookaburras—and their laughter to awake us—a joy.

from Carnarvon by camel trains which, with their long wagons, needed plenty of room to turn around. We arrived at the motel with enough time to continue the work I had begun dictating to Ann in the car, and to deal with the daily yards of faxes awaiting me in the motel; for Hilary to walk 6 km by the river along the dunes; and for Murray to perform his task every evening of cleaning the car. He also had time for a walk to survey the property scene. These breaks from the road, allowed for in the route planning, were a most helpful contribution to RolleroundOz, which was necessarily a concentrated tour.

Next day, on, still north, but turning east towards the end of the day around that bulge in Australia's west coast to reach our destination of Port Hedland. We crossed the Gascoyne River. The river bed is broad, and the bridge long. That day the river was but a sluggish trickle twenty feet below us. The metal barriers either side of the wooden bed of the bridge, we learned, are removed when flood threatens. This relieves the pressure on the bridge of the driving water and the heavy debris it carries, and helps preserve the structure. The Gascoyne is just north of Carnarvon. For many hundreds of kilometres north and east below the Pilbara and Kimberley Ranges, we were to see hundreds of signs saying 'Floodway'. A salt lake stretching well over 100 km lay between the road and the sea. Near its north end is Minilya Roadhouse. We found it sandbagged. Although this defence was against floods, it recalled for me World War II during the London Blitz. Sadly, we lacked the time for the long diversion to Exmouth. Similarly, we had had to deny ourselves a tourist diversion to feed dolphins at Monkey Mia, south of Carnarvon; but we were making good progress up this long coast.

It was a quarter to nine that morning when we crossed the Tropic of Capricorn. Nearby were odd clumps of purple wildflowers; beyond, silver-gold grasses were rippling in the wind like the sea at dawn. There were large red anthills shaped like old English circular haystacks. Such traffic as there was seemed all to be cars pulling caravans.

The next roadhouse was Nanutarra. On the dry sand around the petrol pumps a boat was moored to a post.

Sandbags were not enough there. The place was dusty dry for miles around but the boat had been used only some five months earlier, as we learned from graphic photographs of that, the latest in an unremitting series of floods. Life in the outback is rugged, physical and tough in such a wild mixture of ways. It was at Nanutarra that we saw a parked four-wheel drive vehicle registered in the ACT. Both it and the Rolls were a long way from their homes, both in Canberra. Sadly, we failed to find the owners.

As the Hamersley Ranges began to be just visible to the east, suddenly, from the middle of nowhere, close to the road, there were rocks with ugly graffiti. A pity. But then, over a gentle rise, and as if heralded by those rocks, were hummocky hills. Again we could enjoy the aptness of the term 'jump-up'. A cloud, an ensemble of yellow and green budgerigars danced out of a roadside bush, and sashayed alongside the Rolls by a rear side window for enough moments of balletic brilliance for Hilary to secure still more marvellous video shots, and at the best angle for the sun to highlight the budgerigars' plumage. The next attraction was a glade of ghost gums seen against many giant crenellations of 'jump-ups'. We could glimpse the salt piles way off at Dampier from the road, on which there were that morning copious quantities of kangaroo meat for the increasing number of carnivorous feeders. The land here produced scrub and tussocky grass. Most of the few, scattered clumps of trees had been affected by fires—but not, happily, those deathly pale ghost gums.

We crossed the Hamersley Iron railway line. From an earlier, flying visit, Hilary and I recalled its 2.6 km long train—the world's longest—and its impressive simulator for driver training. We stopped for a lunch of the ubiquitous toasted sandwiches at Karratha Roadhouse. Murray's daughter Emma is in the Federal Public Service and worked for a while in Karratha. Beyond Karratha, we thought some hills looked a little like Scottish moors.

We drove by Aboriginal communities and talked of Yagan's head. Following serious misdemeanours and prison, Yagan was transported from Queensland to Perth by the then Colonial Government, with an eye to his rehabilitation. However, he escaped from his new prison, and a hefty price was put on his head. This great rogue and outlaw was eventually betrayed and shot for the reward by a farmhand from whom he had sought food near the Swan River. Yagan's head was cut off, and later smoked in a burnt-out stump of a tree. The body was buried. Eventually, the head was obtained by the authorities of the day and later sent to the UK where it became an item of museum interest. A hundred or so years later, curators in Liverpool Museum in England decided the head had deteriorated so much that it should be given a decent burial. This was done, in a common grave in nearby Everton Cemetery. In the mid-1990s Ken Colbung, who had researched the story, was in touch with academics and others in England. Ken, an Aboriginal leader from the Swan River and no mean politician, sought, with other Elders, the return of the head—so that it could be reunited with the body and so that the spirit could therefore rest. This belief or sentiment is, of course, by no means restricted to Aboriginal communities.

It is well understood, too, that there is an international tradition of outlaws, even murderers, becoming heroes in their own people's eyes. The British authorities had no objection in principle to the removal of the skull; but a serious practical problem arose. Some of the families of still-born babies buried in the common grave later than and above Yagan's skull had to be asked if they objected. One or two did, and that prevented the removal of Yagan's head because, the experts told us, this could not be done without disturbing the remains above Yagan's. The risk of such disturbance was the reason for the requirement to consult the families.

It had been a task of mine to explain the situation to the Western Australian Aboriginal community concerned. I had attempted that in a polite but not always easy two-hour meeting with elders, including Ken Colbung. I also invited Ken Colbung to visit the UK, and Everton Cemetery in particular. Dressed in his trade-mark long curly hair and coloured head-band, Ken duly went to the UK for a programme organised by the Foreign and Commonwealth Office. He also made himself known to the Australian Prime Minister (who was then visiting London), in Battersea Park, where John Howard and I laid wreaths at an RAAF memorial stone. John Howard undertook to do what he could to help. The British authorities also pursued other technical possibilities and eventually discovered a way to enter the grave from the side and remove Yagan's head without disturbing the other remains above it. With co-operation between both governments, and technical help from Welsh miners, this was done. Things later went a little sour on the publicity front; and there was some discussion within the Aboriginal community near Perth over who should and who should not escort the head home, for example. The story was still not entirely resolved when we were discussing it on the road to Port Hedland. But Yagan's head was returned to Yagan's descendants in Western Australia. I hope there is no more difficulty.

•

We paused in historic Roebourne. We noted the solid old church, the hospital and the brick jail. Hilary and I had flown over this Aboriginal community in a small aeroplane. It was good now to stop and chat, especially with happy children riding scramble motor bikes on dirt roads. At the petrol station, which looked a little glum with its barred windows, the atmosphere was positive and cheerful. A caged galah called Cecil looked surprisingly content with life. A noticeboard among the Aboriginal murals gave the weather forecast: 'Hot, Hot, Hot and Damned Hot'.

A few miles further along, a group of stockmen and one superbly hatted stockwoman were conferring on horseback. They exchanged waves with us. I fancied that they admired the Rolls, but probably dismissed it because only half a dozen sheep could be fitted in the back. The landscape was now painted in pale shades of Australian greens and golds. Three camels sat, perhaps contemplating their Afghan heritage. Whatever it was, they seemed utterly content with themselves and disdainful of the rest of the world. We doubted they were wild.

We found our motel in Port Hedland. The window in our room looked north across the sea. We counted eleven ships waiting to enter port. Bulk carriers, no doubt, queuing to collect iron-ore. Only partly by design, and more by good fortune, Murray met his next-door Canberra neighbours and went out to dinner with them. He had hoped to see them in Broome, so this was an early bonus. Ann and I did some work. Hilary wrote postcards to grandchildren.

Four days after Perth (a long coastline indeed, this), and after a quick dawn seaside Sunday walk to admire the red fire-ball which arose in the east, we left Port Hedland en route for Broome. The early sun dramatically illuminated a scarlet carpet of Sturt Desert Peas. They recalled the fields of poppies in England, France and Flanders. A little later, a range of jutting hills, glimpsed on the horizon through straggly bush, looked to Hilary like a giant-sized toy wooden train.

We soon drove through another Aboriginal community. A score or so of men and boys preferred sleeping bags in the soft, sandy, dry riverbed to their houses. We well saw why: in the warm night before, the stars had recalled Juliet's image of Romeo. A little farther on, a car was parked twenty paces off the road, the boot and four doors open, all surrounded by the debris of a Saturday night party—including two souls soundly sleeping where they had fallen. We were less sure that those two had noticed Banjo Paterson's 'wondrous glory of the everlasting stars'.

This was hot dry country indeed. It was red. The sheep were pink. The hills of iron-ore exuded red as they oxidised. Any rain was noted on blackboards at petrol stations. Solar-powered telephone relay stations were scattered about this apparently deserted land. The few animals were seeking shelter from the climbing sun. The dry landscape was brilliantly lit by the sun and its reflections off the dramatic cloud formations. Once we had left those hot hills of minerals we were on the edge of the Great Sandy Desert.

The Rolls's air-conditioning system worked effortlessly, silently, perfectly. Gratitude abounded for the best in British engineering. (Rolls-Royce and Bentley Motor Cars have since been sold to Volkswagen, against competition from BMW and a British group. So highly valued is the marque that separately, BMW have bought the Rolls-Royce name—the trademark—from Rolls-Royce Aerospace. I trust that both Volkswagen and BMW will remember that financial ownership is not necessarily the same as the original provenance of intellectual property, nor the same as workmanship and craftsmanship. I wish the companies all success in continuing to produce, in Great Britain, the world's best motor cars.)

The evening before, we had seen kangaroos the colour of sand, some of them with cream-coloured waistcoats for camouflage among the dry grasses. As we drove towards Broome we saw a few sheep and cattle but no sign of kangaroos, not even of their demise on the road. We saw and admired the spectacular Australian skies with high striated clouds subtly and economically decorating the blue half sphere. We saw more clouds of green budgerigars. We saw the sand dunes of the Eighty Mile Beach to the west. And we saw hay-coloured grass tufts on red earth or on burned areas which brought dot painting again to mind. Inevitably, but jarringly, we also saw discarded but, in that climate, barely rusting cars.

We pulled into the Sandfire Flat Roadhouse. We saw exactly why Leichhardt had named this spot for the sandy hills there which, reflecting the sun, appeared to be on fire. So strong was the colour and so dramatic was this landscape that it seemed only right that the Sandfire Flat Roadhouse should have peacocks and peahens in the way other roadhouses have families of dogs. The petrol pump attendant recognised the car and us from a Western Australia newspaper picture. She was another bright girl taking a break from the slog of study, and learning a great deal about life around her country.

As we neared Broome, the wide open spaces seemed to become a little kinder to the flora. Perhaps it was the influence of the Fitzroy River system beyond Broome. At all events, a few small pockets of welcome wildflowers appeared here and there. But why would someone turn a road white line marking into a swastika?

We drove into Broome to find even the pearl shops closed on Sunday afternoon. This was the last day of the Shinju Matsuri Festival, which to us signalled the Asian connections the pearling trade had brought to Broome. By way of extra celebration, our motel/hotel, The Mangrove, was to be host that evening to *Opera Under the Stars*, a performance of opera extracts by three Chinese-Australian tenors.

As we registered at the hotel, we asked for tickets for the performance. It had been fully booked for months. Later, after I had received permission to shelter the Rolls at the back of the hotel, I went back to it to retrieve some papers I needed. The hotel owner Ken Fitzgerald, a farmer from the south of Western Australia, was admiring the car. We fell into conversation, and he later found room and most kindly invited us to a brilliant musical evening, to which people had come from all over Australia. The tenors' singing was superb. They occasionally offered a gentle and respectful parody, not an imitation, of the other Three, which drew gasps and applause from a captivated audience. This was a marvellous Western Australia occasion at which we were most fortunate to be present. A post-performance party lit by flares and candles in the tropical house of the organiser of *Opera Under the Stars* completed a day of contrast and contentment. It also marked another significant stage in this enthralling drive around this country we knew we liked greatly, and were beginning to love rather seriously.

Outside Westminster House, Canberra, on day one for a formal picture before the tour began.

Ready to roll with Murray in the back seat for a change.

A well-graded road leads to Blinman, South Australia

An 1860s photograph of Peg-leg Blinman and family on a wall of the North Blinman Hotel.

The first Blinman hotel trading on copper mining success in the 1860s.

Lady Carrick (nee Blinman) capturing on video the South Australian 'town' founded by a possible relative, Peg-leg Blinman. The Rolls Royce stands outside the hotel where a bush butty is kept behind the bar.

Plotting our position by the Spirit of Ecstasy.

6 Broome to Darwin

Day 15 began with Broome hardly visible under a morning sea mist. As we drove east to rejoin the Great Northern Highway, the mist began to ease and a few feeble rays of low sun gently illuminated countless cobwebs among the trees of, quite obviously, fairyland. By contrast, as we escaped the mist, there were suddenly acres of scorched trees: a former fairyland, although regenerating too, as the shoots that would become leaves pushed bravely through the charcoal. Then, an austere grove of ghost gums. The morning had begun well.

A road sign proclaimed proudly, but also warned, 'Road Trains 50 Metres Long'. The road trains were indeed a potent force. In this region where cattle roam freely, the morning also presented us with the sight of dead bullocks and other meat—a feral pig, a couple of bilbies. And carnivores cavorting on the carcasses. As we drove deeper into the Fitzroy River system the countryside became insistently more fecund. There were boab trees,

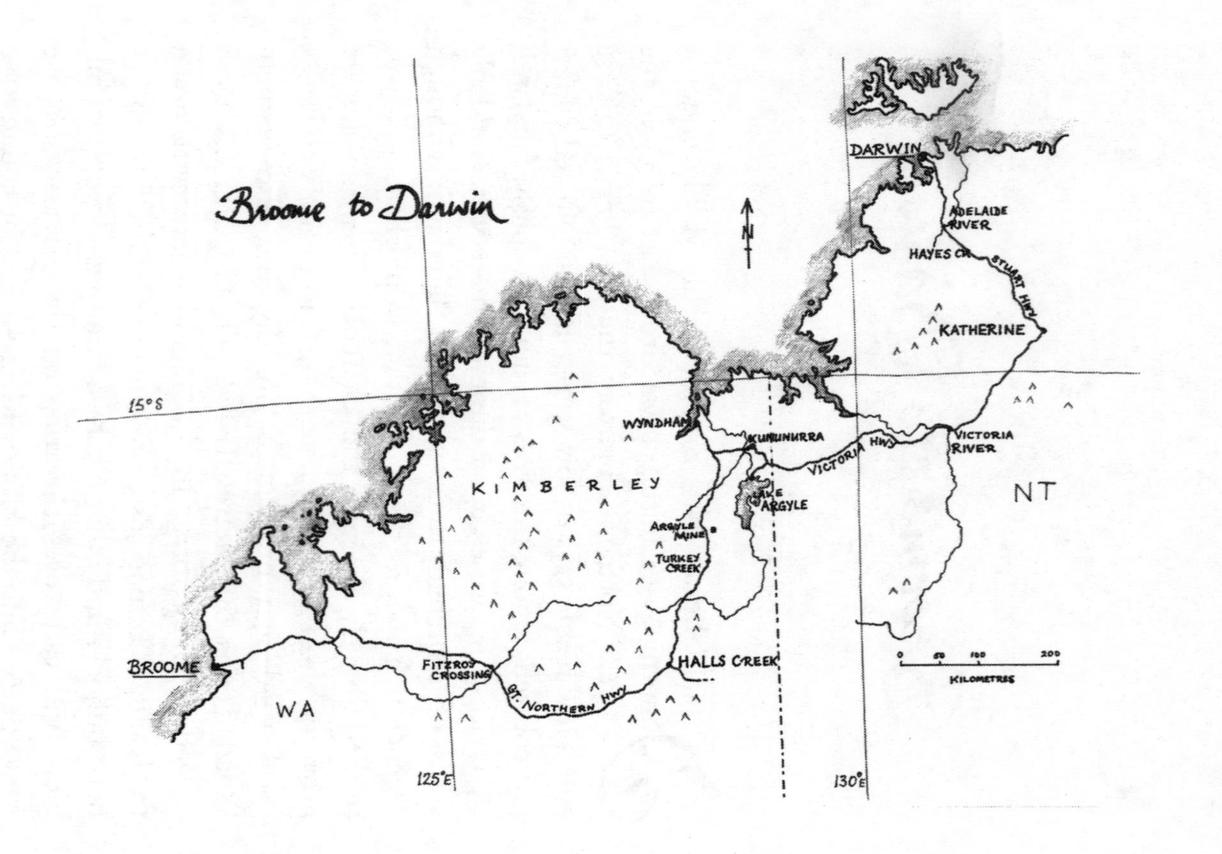
Broome to Darwin
N
DARWIN
ADELAIDE RIVER
HAYES CR
STUART HWY
KATHERINE
15°S
WYNDHAM
KUNUNURRA
VICTORIA HWY
VICTORIA RIVER
KIMBERLEY
LAKE ARGYLE
ARGYLE MINE
TURKEY CREEK
NT
BROOME
FITZROY CROSSING
HALLS CREEK
GT. NORTHERN HWY
WA
125°E
130°E
0
50
100
200
KILOMETRES

Australian Trees

The variety of eucalyptus trees is astonishing. Salmon gums with delicate pink bark, notably but not only in Western Australia; aptly named ghost gums in many regions; majestic jarrah and karri in Western Australia; and tall, old, elegant classic eucalypts enhancing our Canberra garden all impressed us mightily. That garden also boasts an oak from Winston Churchill's Chartwell planted by Robert Menzies, and trees planted by Margaret Thatcher, Princess Alexandra and others (including a claret ash with love from Hilary). With all her deserts, Australia is rich with trees and shrubs—fat boabs grow where growth seems unlikely; Tasmanian trees are particularly varied and lush; the east coast jacarandas are a unique blue; and it is said that a wattle flowers somewhere in Australia every day of the year. Parliament House in Canberra is properly rich with Australian woods.

which hold so much water and sustenance. There were termite mounds like turreted castles. There was a large billabong with gum trees reflected in its still water. The road rose to avoid the deepest of the floods the area clearly suffered. The evidence, including the water marks on the trees, was clear. There were wildflowers again, but far fewer than south-west of the Great Sandy Desert. We crossed the Fitzroy River. Here were more hardy cattle and sheep. There was almost no traffic; but we passed and, after lunch, passed again a group of Aborigines travelling by 'ute', probably, we thought, to Halls Creek. When we first saw them, three were soundly and apparently even comfortably asleep in the back of the 'ute'. When we caught up with them again after our lunch, they might have been having theirs: at least they were taking an evidently refreshing drink.

During lunch at the Fitzroy Roadhouse, we spoke with some young Australian four-wheel adventurers with a determined-looking vehicle, complete with snorkel. They told us they had been in water up to the roof. We hadn't seen anything that deep: they had probably found it well off-road in the Kimberleys.

Fitzroy Crossing is one of two points where the river crosses the road. It is at the southern end of the Leopold Downs and the King Leopold Ranges, which lead northwards to the Kimberleys. The surrounding countryside looked like the savannah of Africa. The blue sky was tricked out that day with fluffy white clouds. On the ground were small anthills looking like Moslem grave markers. We skirted still more of the Kimberleys, enjoyed both them and the sight of sleek and elegant wild horses in the evening sun, and came to Halls Creek. We drove on a little of the Duncan Road, a dirt road, and there savoured the red hills with scattered green bushes, and their evocation, once again, of dot painting.

People had said we shouldn't stay in Halls Creek: it was too remote; there were risks. They were wrong. Not about the remoteness. Nor in the implication that Halls Creek was different. We found it a township heavily dominated numerically by Aborigines, and a cheerful and helpful place. The motel was friendly, welcoming and helpful. We had been advised to make contact with the police. This we did in a smart efficient police station, where the sergeant on duty, a tall, pleasant, obviously able and smartly dressed young man, told us there really would be no problem in Halls Creek. He added, laughing, that it was not pay day. We had a good dinner in a busy and convivial restaurant. The car was perfectly safe outside our spacious, clean and comfortable motel rooms.

Radio, press and television coverage of RolleroundOz seemed to be growing. More importantly, it was positive. But for us to be called 'royalty' on Halls Creek Radio next morning was a bit much. No doubt the presenter had his tongue firmly in his cheek. However, quite often during RolleroundOz I found myself explaining the facts to people who genuinely did not know that in Australia I did not and could not represent Her Majesty. I represented the British Government. The Queen's representatives are of course the Governor-General and the Governors. And in Australia, Her Majesty is Queen of Australia, not of the UK. Perhaps that, and much else about the Constitution, may become clearer as a result of the Constitutional Convention held in February 1998. So I do not criticise the joking radio commentator in Halls Creek. But the headline writer in the *Sydney Morning Herald* who wrote 'Queen's Man Takes a Roller 'round Australia' should really have known better. I am of course a Queen's man, and represented Her Majesty when serving as Ambassador in Indonesia. But in Australia I was a Queen's man only as a UK subject.

•

Next morning, on northwards, through an increasingly warm and watered red, brown and green landscape. Marvellous hills, jumbled rocky outcrops. A concreted ford across a river now dry but, when full, evidently capable of shifting massive boulders. The anthills here looked like neglected gravestones in an old English churchyard, overgrown with creepers and trees. The flora was different again and included bushes with bright yellow flowers but no leaves, and monstrous boabs. It was now hot, and it was very much the dry season. We passed by a bustling cattle muster. Travelling west, an extra wide load of oil rig machinery reminded us that we were not far from the natural gas resources under the sea, off Karratha, Port Hedland, and further north into the Timor Sea. Just the other side of the Kimberleys, the land sloped down to the Timor Sea. I recalled the successful conclusion of the treaty negotiations between Australia and Indonesia that had facilitated exploitation of those resources in the Timor Sea. I recalled, too, the photograph of the signing by the two Foreign Ministers, Gareth Evans and Ali Alatas, in an aeroplane high above the Timor Sea. If I recalled aright, Gareth and Pak Ali were jokingly arm-wrestling on the table between them.

On the ground, we too were among serious resource country. Beyond the Bungle Bungles and not far to the east of the Great Northern Highway was the Argyle Diamond Mine. Hilary and I had spent three days there, learning a good deal about this British investment, the techniques of diamond mining, and interesting and successful human resource management methods. We had arrived there by Twin Otter from Kununurra, flying over

Lake Argyle in a crimson sunset. The sky, the lake, the hills around and the islands that had once been hilltops were all crimson. Next day, the temperature in the shade was 47°C, and I had thought again of that sunset: I don't think I shall ever forget it.

The Bungle Bungles now behind us, we continued north, purring away through marvellous hills. We noted an escarpment with a line of trees at its top. The light behind them caused the trees to resemble a lace frill above a stern hospital matron's cap of Victorian times. Small eucalyptus trees dotted here and there contrasted with their rich uncles living grandly and standing tall by rivers and creeks.

We stopped for coffee at Turkey Creek where, parked by the roadhouse, was a cattle road train with three two-storey trailers, packed with Brahmins. We hoped the driver would finish his own refreshment quickly, and at least hose down the restless, noisily pawing beasts before they became distressed.

Over coffee we discussed Ann's enviable plan to leave us at Kununurra to take some holiday and return to the Bungle Bungles. We agreed that the Kimberleys, which Hilary and I had seen before only from the air, excelled their reputation for grandeur. They were majestic, long, rugged and beautiful—all at once. As we drove on, the Durack and O'Donnell Ranges to the left and the Carr Boyd Range to the right seemed ready to 'volley and thunder'—though we were hardly the Light Brigade. Birds on nests in leafless trees were presumably waiting for the wet season and leaves to make their nests less obvious.

We crossed the Dunham River. It was almost a surprise to find some water in it, although this was the region of the Ord River Scheme, just over the hills to the right, and of water management on a huge scale. We recalled the devotion and skill of the agriculturalists and other experts we had met earlier when visiting the Scheme. I had been much taken by their support for an imaginative mango orchard scheme for the Aborigines of the area. There must be many similar schemes, but I was so struck by this one that I thought it right to raise the subject with Lois O'Donoghue, then Chairman of ATSIC (see also chapter 3). I hope the scheme succeeded.

It was odd, and a reminder of how far north we were, to see palm trees among the scrub. Unlike mangoes, they did not need special irrigation and management schemes. Here and there, burn-offs marred the landscape. But they would do so only temporarily, and the colours of the remaining red earth and some new growth were enhanced by their backcloth of black ash.

At the north-east edge of the Kimberleys, we ignored the right turn to Kununurra and pressed on to Wyndham. Fifty kilometres earlier, the satellite telephone had rung with confirmation of our Wyndham rendezvous with the *Current Affair* television crew. I had been keen to visit this seriously remote port ever since learning of it from the Captain of the British naval ship HMS *Sheffield*, who had taken his ship there during Exercise Kangaroo 95, to 'retake' the port which had 'fallen' into the hands of the 'enemy'. The British Captain and crew had never experienced anywhere so remote.

On the outskirts of Wyndham there is a brown and apparently scarcely used golf course. Ditto racecourse. The nearby Aboriginal communities looked relatively poor and run-down. The maps and the guide books say of Wyndham, 'Meatworks'. They should say, 'Burned and abandoned Meatworks'. We drove to a look-out called The Bastion at the top of the hill above Wyndham. It was a humbling, sobering, almost surreal experience to gaze some 240° around and over many hundreds of kilometres of desolate wasteland. Hamlet's 'stale, flat and unprofitable' came to mind. Five rivers debouch there, in a vast grey-brown delta. Mud and water are the same colour, and stretch to the far horizons. All was hazy in the heat. Presumably the fishing was good off Wyndham, at least for the crocodiles.

There was not much else to see apart from the meatworks burned a few years before. But the small port was of interest. We saw almost no sign of human activity; some of automation. By the evidence of its unusual equipment, and that of a waiting Norwegian ship, the port specialised in exporting live cattle. As we watched, that road train so laden with the unhappy Brahmins we had seen at Turkey Creek drove along the short quay to the ship. The Brahmins were to be loaded for Indonesia, where they would probably be fattened on pineapple pulp for six weeks before slaughter. In a way it seemed right that the only vegetation near the port was a group of very dead boab trees. But then, incongruously, it occurred to me that the very live HMS *Sheffield* must have moved alongside this same quay. The ship would have noted those same expired boabs—and the wild remoteness of Wyndham.

The Wyndham petrol station, below The Bastion, was run by a Swedish couple and Jessie their Jack Russell puppy, who became a firm friend and evidently found deep satisfaction in chewing on Ann's fingers. There we met the television crew from Perth. They had flown to Kununurra and driven to Wyndham in a four-wheel drive vehicle. They set to work filming, including our visit to the port.

We had lunch with the crew in the only pub near the port. Fish, of course. Good folk and a quiet, pleasant pub. But, I thought, not quite what some of the crew of HMS *Sheffield* would have wanted in a good run ashore. Over lemon, lime and bitters and lunch, we planned more filming, including off-road on a bone-dry, cracked and heat-shimmering mud flat. As we left Wyndham to find the mud flat, a mini-corroboree began under gum trees. As Murray and the Rolls-Royce displayed their skills on the mud flat, Hilary once again filmed the filming; and we took some excellent stills Rolls-Royce might like. On the way to drop Ann at her hotel in Kununurra, there was some more filming, including of a proudly British and venerable Mini-Minor which happily hooted its horn as it overtook the Rolls-Royce while we were driving slowly to help the filming. We wondered whether the television crew had laid on the Mini, or whether this was serendipity. Certainly, that happy little scene was used in the eventual television report. We said goodbye and thanks to Ann at her hotel. She later told us of the super time she had had on holiday in the Bungle Bungles and other excursions. We drove on through dramatic hills at sunset to Lake Argyle, the crew filming as we drove, and Hilary filming them.

The television crew and we spent the night at Lake Argyle Tourist Village. This is a motel imaginatively made from modified construction camp units. The camp was for the Ord Dam whose nearly completed stages we had seen from the air two years before. The motel was run by a relaxed outback character who fished in the lake for the motel kitchen. He complained that I had run the motel out of rolls of fax paper with messages and questions from the High Commission and Consulates.

Just after we arrived, so did a coach-load of tourists from Adelaide who had flown up to Darwin and thence travelled by coach. While I worked on the faxes, Hilary went to the reception desk for some fruit juice. There she found one of the ladies of Adelaide complaining bitterly that she was having a raw deal. She likened the motel to a backpackers' dosshouse, and threatened to leave, along with the rest of the coach-load. They had come to see the Kimberleys and the wildflowers further south, and they were not going to put up with accommodation like this. The proximate cause of her rage was, she complained, that she had seen a rat in her room. Hilary and I concluded later that the animal was probably one of those little marsupials peculiar to the area, and harmless. Hilary left with her fruit juice during the height of the altercation, but was overtaken and engaged in conversation by the lady in the gardens among the motel units. Hilary could offer no real sympathy because she felt we were cleanly and adequately housed—even though she had to kneel before the bed to type a fax on the computer. When they reached our unit, there was the Rolls-Royce beyond it, and Murray, naturally, cleaning it. As Hilary came into our room, the lady from Adelaide went to interrogate Murray. Twenty minutes later, the relaxed outback character arrived with a bottle of wine and much thanks to

Hilary, Murray and especially the Rolls-Royce, for having saved him the ignominy and financial loss of the ladies departing in their coach for Kununurra. Just on balance, I was rather glad that the television crew were then out reconnoitring sites for filming interviews at dawn the next day!

We had dinner with the crew, preceded by a short interview at the bar. The crew seemed a little surprised at the canteen-like arrangements for dinner, but tucked in, and joined in a chatty evening.

Next morning about dawn, we filmed interviews on the road across the dam wall. The exercise was enhanced by sparkling early morning light illuminating fabulous scenery. We took some more stills of the Rolls with dramatic backgrounds. Then Wayne, the intrepid cameraman from the Perth rush hour, was strapped to the outside of a helicopter, his feet on the skis and holding his heavy video camera before him, to film the Rolls as we wound our way through the steep-sided hills above Lake Argyle and the Ord Dam. That made fine photography. Hilary had the easy task of filming the helicopter filming us as we drove: the result looked like one of the highpoints in a James Bond epic, without the sound effects. As we wound our way through the eroded, tiered, red rocky outcrops, the only concern I had was whether the pilot would see the occasional wire strung across the gorge. He saw every one, and hopped over each like a jack-rabbit, which must have been extra fun for Wayne as he struggled with his heavy camera.

•

We waved farewell to Wayne, rejoined the Victoria Highway, and drove on towards Katherine. We passed through the Western Australia Quarantine Station and into the Northern Territory. We had now driven over 10 000 km—over half way. And we heard on the radio that the England Schoolboys had beaten their Australian counterparts at rugby union: another *new*IMAGE!

There would be lots more of the Northern Territory to come in the next five days, including the State elections. Meanwhile we could appreciate the considerable geographical and geological change this artificial straight line on the map, the State border, happens to mark at this latitude. It was still hot. But now the flies began to buzz. Small birds of prey circled on thermals. There were still the golden spinifex and the green gum leaves, but the canyons, gullies and crags had a starker beauty than their counterparts in Western Australia. There were still burn scars; but near Victoria River two large fires were raging. Although we had seen Victoria River on the map and read of it, it was nonetheless a surprise in this dry heat to find it a broad deep expanse of steadily flowing, life-giving water. The red soil here was brighter. We were closely conscious of it as we had to drive on dirt roads for some kilometres while road work was in progress. Road dust and dirt invaded the well in which the petrol cap sits. The dust found its way around the edges of the well's elegant cover, but of course never reached the tank or the fuel. There was never a speck of dust inside the car or in the boot. That petrol-pump attendant had it right: Mr Royce certainly did a fine job!

To European eyes, the colour of the red soil of the

Northern Territory is that of a bright flag rather than gentle nature. But while it had been the work of man to squash the snake and the two bilbies we saw just along the road, it was hardly a gentle nature who arranged for the birds of prey and scavengers to squabble so fiercely as they fed voraciously on the mess on the road. But they did clear it up eventually. Now, at midday, the occasional Brahmin cattle sought some solace from the sun under sparse gums. A few Brahmins had found a little water. It was almost shocking to see a tired traveller a little later, dousing his head under a wide-open tap in a roadhouse forecourt.

Unusually, there was some traffic for a few miles. We found ourselves in company with two vehicles, one from Tasmania and one from Victoria. All three of us were far from home. We squeezed in a quick educational side-trip to Katherine Gorge Visitors' Centre. As ever, there was not enough time to see the Gorge itself, which can be visited only by boat. Back on the road, we also saw rather a lot that day of a convertible Saab—just like our younger son's. We stayed overnight at Katherine, the Northern Territory's third largest town and the nearest town to RAAF Tindal.

We enjoyed having the driver of the Saab as a dinner companion that evening. He was a consultant from Perth who owned land past which we had driven south of Greenough, WA. He had sold some of the land to pay for this trip. He told us that he thought Hilary had driven too gently along the temporary red dirt roads by the miles of road works. (She had driven at the posted speed limit!) We discussed road conditions and routes as if we were engaged in a rally. And we were to see the Saab and its driver again in Darwin, where he told us he had hoped to sell the car, but could not get a good price for it. Instead, he was going to have it freighted home to Perth, while he flew.

We had changed our watches, for the umpteenth time it felt, on entry to the Northern Territory. So Day 18 dawned rather later than usual for us. By 7.30 am, a sultry sky accurately foretold a hot heavy day. The air-conditioned splendour of the Rolls strongly suggested that this may just be the only way to see Australia. We headed north to Darwin, driving through a long-lasting slow burn area. The debris at the feet of the gum trees smouldered determinedly. Seen from a distance, the smoke looks brown, but seen close up, it was surprisingly blue smoke that drifted lazily through the trees. The blue, of course, is the same as that of the eucalyptus vapour which impregnates and colours the hills of Victoria and New South Wales. Presumably, the slow burn process prepares the ground to encourage the new shoots to grow when the rains come in the Wet.

It was a pleasant surprise to hear British yachtsman Tony Bullimore on the radio. We recalled his extraordinary rescue by the RAN, RAAF and the Maritime Search Coordination Office in Canberra we had visited. We recalled also how Tony Bullimore came to the High Commission in a wheelchair as a guest at a party. His frostbitten feet prevented him from walking. He must have enjoyed that balmy Canberra evening in February. The party was out of doors. Prime Minister John Howard and Deputy Prime Minister Tim Fischer came too, for the launch of *new*IMAGES. John Howard also re-opened the re-architectured and refurbished British High Commission, and Tim Fischer unveiled a sculpture in tribute to the shared sacrifices of Australians and Britons in the defence of freedom. I presented Tony Bullimore with a new passport, granted and issued because it was too far to go back and retrieve his old one!

The Northern Territory termite hills are the largest in Australia. Some have the name 'cathedral': their architecture is on a grand scale, but intricate too. Salmon gums in the morning sun have now imprinted themselves as one of our enduring memories of Australia. The thought of them brings a glow of pleasure as I write.

It is still hard for mere Europeans to quite come to terms with all these hectares of burnt landscape and the theory behind the burning. Practice seems to be a mixture of folklore, modern science and hope. Natural recovery from natural disaster is one thing, but can invasive techniques really do better? Perhaps they can, if they pre-empt disaster. Can we really tell?

•

Hayes Creek Roadhouse has a new and different sign: 'Tank and Tummy Stop'. We did.

We reached the Adelaide River where, three years earlier, on the first of our several visits to Darwin, we had cruised the river and watched jumping crocodiles. This is an extraordinary exercise in which raw meat is attached to the end of long poles and suspended off a river boat. As the crocodile rises the long pole is pivoted so that the meat is elevated. The well practised crocodiles leap high out of the water to grab the food. We were glad to obey the strict instructions to stay well inside the boat. Tourist attraction, yes. Careful exercise in wooing the crocodiles in the wild, yes. Gimmick, perhaps; but a good one.

And so to Darwin, of which we are fond, mostly because of the people, but also because of the two-season dramatic climate and its reminders for us of our four years in Indonesia. Then there are Darwin's economic and political connections with Indonesia, which has the only home-based Consulate-General in Darwin, and a substantial one at that. And there is a nostalgic connection with my service 25 years ago in Singapore when, as Head of Chancery there, I had some responsibility for the then British Government Wireless Relay Station move from Singapore to Darwin. It seemed a good idea at the time, when we were withdrawing British troops east of Suez, and the necessary real estate would no longer be available in Singapore. We achieved the move successfully, just less than eighteen months before the new station was completely wiped out by Cyclone Tracy. It has always given us mixed feelings to see the Darwin site, and to hear tales of the cyclone from Northern Territorians who experienced it. And then there is the RAF/RAAF connection from World War II. The RAF Spitfire Squadron which fought with distinction and success in the defence of Darwin against the Japanese Airforce is well remembered in the Northern Territory and is now commemorated there.

Darwin has a new and imposing parliament building. It had been much criticised as too large and expensive for a Territory of only some 171 000 people. As I told an ABC radio interviewer in Alice Springs a few days after the building was opened, the parliaments of New South Wales and Victoria, for example, are grand, imposing, expensive and had been built when their populations were much smaller. This was a proud Territory building, a modern statement of pride and hope; and a building which would be used by Territorians, not just parliamentarians. And I admired the architecture, too. The ABC interviewer thought I was in a very small minority, on all counts. But the fuss has died away, and the building seems widely accepted and well used (including, kindly, for one of the thirteen travelling copies of that British photographic exhibition discussed in chapter 2).

Darwin has grown remarkably and well in the three years we have known it. We were privileged to be allowed to sit with the members on the floor of the House at the first session in that parliament building. Chief Minister Marshall Perron's speech on that occasion was a well researched, excellently written and delivered historical review, and an important statement of the case for statehood. As I recall, the then Chief Minister spoke for some 40 minutes, interrupted only once by a mild comment from the Opposition. Marshall Perron's speech that day made no immediate discernible difference to progress towards statehood, but will, I think, prove to have been a key contribution to the statehood I believe will eventually be achieved.

Hilary and I first met the present Chief Minister, Shane Stone, when Philip Flood, then Australian Ambassador in Indonesia and later Secretary of the Department of Foreign Affairs and Trade, brought him to a reception we were holding at the British Residence in Jakarta. The day of Marshall Perron's speech was the second occasion. Shane then button-holed me and lobbied me fast and hard about a possible British investment in the Northern Territory. I immediately added respect to the liking I had felt for this senior Northern Territory minister since our first meeting. Since then, we had become good friends with Josephine and Shane. On the evening of our arrival in Darwin, we had a relaxed and very enjoyable dinner at their house. It was a Thursday night off for the Chief Minister, just two days before his Territory elections. Was it courageous or risky to take such a night off? I imagined Shane's election advisers thought it was both. But it was a Northern Territory thing to do, and Shane Stone's judgment was evidently correct: his party won well on the Saturday. Dinner was great fun: we tried around the table, with only moderate success, to talk of subjects other than politics. We did reminisce about a unique and wonderful fishing expedition Hilary and I and Shane and his son Jack had made one weekend when Josephine was pregnant with Madeleine.

There are new stylish hotels in Darwin, smartly refurbished mayoral offices and good government offices. There are, of course, handsome state-of-the-art new port facilities. And there is al fresco eating on Mitchell Street. The construction industry has benefited from the increase in population consequent on the Armed Forces' move of so many people and so much equipment north. The sense of confidence in Darwin has grown too, almost palpably. We found that the recent decision by the Federal Government to contribute, along with the governments of South Australia and the Northern Territory, to the construction of a railway line from Alice Springs to Darwin, had been greeted there with relief, but with some disappointment too—that the amount Canberra had pledged was not larger. It was 78 years since it had first been 'decided' in principle to complete the south–north railway link. There is an interesting and complex series of politico-economic equations involved in this decision—for taxpayers and governments and for the private sector in Australia and abroad. I personally believe the railway will eventually be constructed. When that happens, it will be an historic moment, and one of particularly significant economic and commercial significance.

The next day, we enjoyed another privilege: lunch with the former Administrator and his family. Austen Asche is an erudite and able raconteur. Valerie and he are engaging hosts. We discussed English language and literature, Indonesia, the railway and much else besides. To our astonishment and delight, Austen Asche served that excellent English white wine we knew so well—Chiddingstone.

We paid the official calls that day, all too briefly but most interestingly renewing our acquaintance with the new Administrator, Neil Conn, and his wife Lesley (Philip Flood's sister). I paid a useful, and for me educational, call on the Chief Justice. And we had another in a series of the always enlightening and entertaining meetings with Lord Mayor George Brown GRBC, this time with Mrs Brown too. GRBC is an unusual (and unofficial) honour. George is an unusual and versatile man. GRBC stands for Grand Rough Bush Carpenter. We learned much of local politics from him; and we talked of that day's newspaper editorial about parrots in the shopping mall, drunk from nectar from the euodia trees. We talked of George's recent resignation from the Planning Committee—he believed he would be more effective outside it. And we talked of the joys of the Rolls-Royce.

The rest of that day was taken up with some office and other work, and a drive through the most impressive new Robinson Barracks. This struck me as a modern high-tech version of one of the tropical paradise barracks we Brits used to have in Singapore and gave to Lee Kuan Yew's government in the early 1970s. But Robinson is the more elegant.

That evening in the Hotel Beaufort we met again, this time unexpectedly, the Western Australia *A Current Affair* television crew. The greeting was of long lost friends. The crew were about to join a patrol vessel, HMAS *Launceston*, for a search for illegal fishermen.

The next day we would leave Darwin, regretfully indeed. Sherry Meakin, Protocol Officer par excellence of the Northern Territory Government, arranged in lightning time and at her initiative a diversion which would enable us to put right a wrong the following morning: we had never seen Kakadu.

7 Darwin to Bundaberg

We left Darwin early, before sun-up, to allow the necessary extra time to fit in the quick trip to Kakadu, with instruction and help so efficiently organised by Sherry Meakin. The sun rose, a fiery red ball which seemed to suit the smell of burn-offs in the air. An eerie mist rose dilatorily from the wetlands, as if to allow us only to glimpse the countless water birds and a pair of green parrots flitting through gum trees in search of breakfast. Two pelicans flew ponderously past a group of pandanus palms. We had seen this peculiar kind of palm tree every day on the road since Albany, WA.

As we crossed the West Alligator River, a couple of crocodiles were quietly awaiting breakfast. At Bowari Visitors' Centre, Senior Project Manager Greg Miles and Chairman of Jabiru Town Council David Norton met us. Greg provided a swift but fascinating and instructive tour of the centre. We left reluctantly, but David Norton kindly accompanied us in the Rolls to Yellow Waters. On the

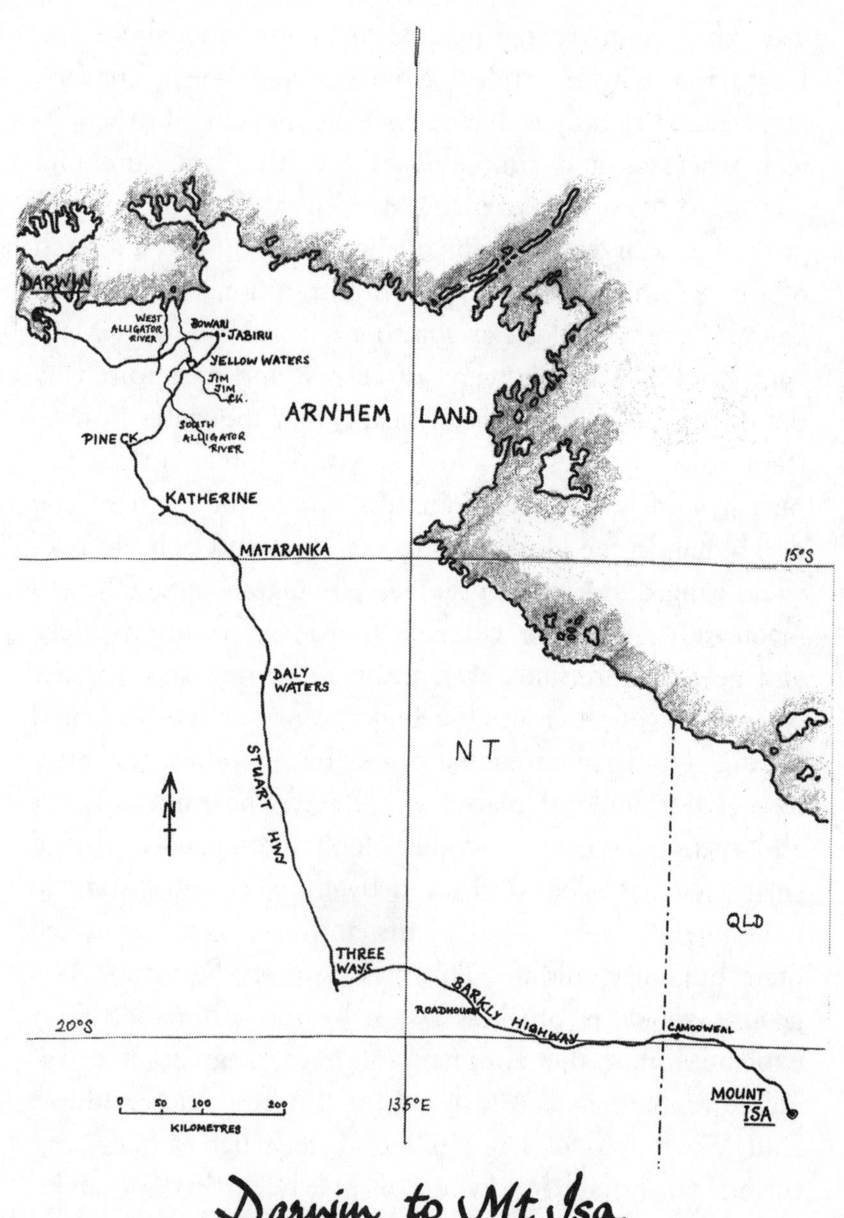

Darwin to Mt Isa

way, we were instructed further, including in local politics. David is a new Australian from Croydon, near London, and seemed rapidly to have become expert in all the political processes and problems of Kakadu, from uranium mining to town management. At Yellow Waters, we were given an unforgettable tour of the Billabong and a stretch of the South Alligator River with traditional owner and Senior Ranger Violet Lawson, her sister Nellie and Manager Terry Reece. We were astounded and enraptured by the quantity and intensity of beauty—of the water flowers (the snowdrop lilies are a lovely example), marsh trees and plants, wild horses and countless other wildlife from the darkly handsome glossy ibis to the swift and delicate bee-eater, from dart birds on the nest to magpie-geese (Violet's favourite), Australian white ibis, sea eagles, kites, ducks and geese galore, and even brolgas—those extraordinary performers of their unique ballet. Terry wisely switched off the already quiet engine of our boat to allow us better to feel this magical place, where even the thieving kites and the malevolent crocodiles looked especially fit and smart. We sat silent and awed by the acres of snowdrop lilies, many other marsh plants and trees, and so much quiet but busy wildlife. This was a watery fairyland. As a goanna took his breakfast walk by the waterside, Terry explained that the abdomen of a local green ant was edible for humans. 'And good for the 'flu,' Violet added. And Violet told of her childhood with her father—venturing on horseback where four-wheel drive vehicles cannot go.

It was hard indeed to leave these people and the wetlands they knew and loved so well. It was hard indeed to leave this breathtaking but also serenely beautiful place and experience.

•

We drove on down the Kakadu Highway. We were unusually quiet after such an unforgettable series of sights and sounds, and so much concentrated beauty. I was also pondering the arguments for and against uranium mining, and the difficulties of national park management. It was comforting that the management was being done by such good and expert people. We joined the Stuart Highway once again at Pine Creek and turned south-east to go through Katherine again, and eventually to Mataranka.

A most unusual place, Mataranka. Perhaps its thermal baths as well as its position just south of a presumed World War II defensive line explains its use during that war as a base and rest camp. Many memorabilia remain. Parts of armoured cars, guns and the detritus of army supplies line the road rather smartly. A World War II airstrip parallels the road closely. Such airstrips are dotted around the Top End landscape. Nearby, that classic of the outback *We of the Never-Never* was written—and lived. We called in at an antique shop cum visitors' centre cum café for a cool drink and delightful conversation with the wise lady owner-philosopher. She told us the family history of an antique piano, and how her mother in Western Australia, on return there from a visit to Mataranka, had the piano despatched across this vast continent of a country, because she thought her grandchildren were ready to learn music. We talked, too, of the Territory elections that day. Living many miles from anywhere at all, this lady was up to date and possessed of well-argued views on local and international politics. As we left, so did she, to do a radio interview for the BBC!

We stayed at Mataranka's roadside inn, which was itself constructed in part from World War II material. The accommodation was basic, but as at Lake Argyle, adequate. The place to eat was the bar. We arrived there about seven in the evening to find a citizen of Mataranka sporting a smart well-trimmed silver beard, wearing a look of world weariness, and sitting on a bar stool, his elbows on the bar, in front of a long line of empties. I asked him how he was. The laconic reply was 'Better now'! This began an amusing evening with a few Matarankans, three other overnighters, and a young lady visitor on a college environmental project. This keen young greenie was wearing her Saturday night black dress, evidently determined to have an exciting time. We did our best for her, including climbing up the bar wall at her behest to pin my business card in one of the few remaining empty spots. We ate a wholesome and hefty dinner at the bar. It had been cooked down the road somewhere and delivered by a lady carrying three large trays at once.

During the entertaining evening, we naturally had to endure a joyful and growing chorus of remarks about English cricket (we had just lost another Test to Australia in England). I explained about the cycles in these things, and how the one certainty was that England would win a Test series…one day. I applauded Australian captain Mark Taylor's recent return to form. I described the rain I had seen in June in London at the Lord's Test, rain which had helped ensure a draw. I recalled former British Prime Minister Alec Douglas-Home's cricketing prayer: 'Oh Lord if there be cricket in Heaven, let there also be rain'. All to no avail. However, in this roadside place, there was much knowledge of vehicles; and admiration for the Rolls-Royce and RolleroundOz eventually took the edge off the caustic comments about English cricket. We ended the evening by watching a good election victory speech by Shane Stone on the television set I was slightly surprised to find in our room.

Next day, Sunday, 31 August, we began the 1251 km drive to Mt Isa before dawn, as a sliver of moon faded and was replaced by an orange-red sun which soon became a sparkling yellow. The early light was superb on salmon gums, and on much else. In the first hour on the road we saw only one vehicle, a three-piece road train we overtook. There were no wildflowers in bloom to be seen, only long golden speargrass, gum trees and Moslem grave-marker anthills. There was less variation in the countryside than across the Nullarbor. This area recalled parts of Zimbabwe and Botswana. We drove on gravel to avoid some miles of road works. We passed many signs to World War II airfields and a few to hospital sites. The radio reception was too poor to hear anything. We supposed that the fact that there were no dead animals on the road was explained by the paucity of vehicles, people and animals.

After Daly Waters, however, the landscape cheered up. There were she-oaks. A few cattle were grazing in a huge paddock: it had to be huge, so sparse was the pasture, if pasture that thin growth could be called. A pelican dried his wings by a small farm dam. It must have been in the dam that he got his wings wet, but was there really enough food around—even for many miles around—for him to live? A World War II prisoner of war camp site was now a caravan park. War-time huts had been converted to holiday accommodation. We wondered who would holiday in somewhere quite so remote: but the very remoteness had its compelling attractions too, and the contrast between, say, living in a Sydney suburb with no view and holidaying here, where one could see for miles across the low scrub and tufty grass, would provide a complete change as well as a rest.

Later, a few straggly wayside wildflowers struggled to bloom as we very gently climbed to rockier ground which gave an even broader view of the barren miles of outback. There was no sign of human habitation. But the barrenness had its colour—50 subtly shifting shades, from pale straw through yellows, oranges and reds to dark green. At Renner Springs, large cattle-mustering areas told a tale of vast areas of cattle and long days of patient mustering. Much further on, we saw the result: a muster of both cattle and their temporary mobile homes, the road trains, on to which stock were being loaded that Sunday morning.

The unremitting flatness of most of this country, and the broad rough tracks cut at angles from the road into the bush to help absorb flood water and preserve the road, inspired a discussion in the car about the resources devoted to flood preparations and pre-emption in Western Australia and the Northern Territory. Different methods had been developed for different conditions, but the evidence assembled of the hazards of drought and flood that Australian outback farmers face, and the thought of early settlers learning of those hazards the hard way, were sobering.

•

Finally, a change of course to the east when we turned left at Three Ways. We turned on to the Barkly Highway, a road we were never to forget. A couple of hundred kilometres along it the satellite telephone rang. An efficient message from Miles in Canberra delivered the shattering news, a little more than an hour after the awful event, of the dreadful death in dreadful circumstances of Diana, Princess of Wales, Dodi al-Fayed and their driver. We were deeply shocked and silent for a while. I then spoke with Deputy High Commissioner Andrew Pocock in Canberra about some practical implications, and to London. The satellite telephone allowed me also to respond to requests for interviews with the ABC and other information media. Already I was learning that Australian reactions and tributes were warm, generous, moving.

I telephoned the Consul-General in Brisbane to ask him to cancel the official dinner we had planned to give the next day in Mount Isa. I thought hard about whether to return to Canberra. We heard the time the National Memorial Service was to take place too late to reach an airport and thence Canberra in time to be present at it. There were several other reasons why I should return, including to talk directly with senior Australian officials and ministers. But all other official business, including this tour, could continue. I was in ready communication with London, Canberra and the Consulates-General, and Andrew was a fine Deputy. There was much to do, but it all could and would be done, and on a fine balance I decided to continue with the tour.

We arrived at the hotel in Mount Isa to find Consul-General Steve Hiscock from Brisbane, faxes and almost total television coverage of the ghastly accident. I did some more interviews. We had a working supper with Steve.

Next morning there were roses in our room and thoughtful, caring cards. I learned of multitudes of floral and other tributes at the High Commission, the Consulates-General and, of course, at gubernatorial and government offices. At a call on hospitable Tony Grady MLA and his wife Sandra, Tony gave us a copy of fine verse by a Queensland poet, who had composed it overnight, in tribute to Diana.

I reflected that some of the constitutional proprieties had been unconsciously judged irrelevant. So they were. The death of Diana, Princess of Wales, was a grievous loss to both Australia and Britain. Hilary and I discussed our having met the Princess in Buckingham Palace, when the two Princes were barely of school age. The Princess of Wales, of course, had been stunning. We both remembered in particular her eyes, more beautiful than the best photographers could ever render. She had starred that evening. We recalled thinking at the time that she had a specially tough row to hoe. It had since become tougher. Hilary and I also discussed the Princess's most recent visit to Australia and how much she had done in so short a time for charity in Sydney: indeed how much she had done in so short and difficult a life for charity and for people around the world. As the next days went by we were to be struck continually by the almost overwhelming emotional outpouring of Australian shock and grief; and we were glad to be able to be a little involved.

•

Our official calls in Mt Isa with Steve Hiscock continued. We had a good conversation with the Deputy Mayor, in the Mayor's absence. We found Mt Isa Mine Manager Steve Bywater supervising inevitable reviews, but in fine form. Darcy Redman was especially helpful, with good advice in many practical ways.

We went to the School of the Air headquarters, where Karin, Darcy's wife, is the principal. Year Seven were studying Government under their able teacher, Mr Cooper. I was invited to join in, and did so keenly. The children, scattered over thousands of miles, were eager and bright. They had good ideas and refreshing views. I admired the way Mr Cooper ensured that they all had a share of air-time, and all were brought to think. The disadvantages of separation in education had been reduced enormously by this excellent school. In this lesson, I think it was I who learned the most—about life in isolated farms and stations, and about outback attitudes to government —local, State and Federal.

In between the official calls, I did many more interviews by telephone. We remembered to send a fax on his retirement to Returned and Services League then

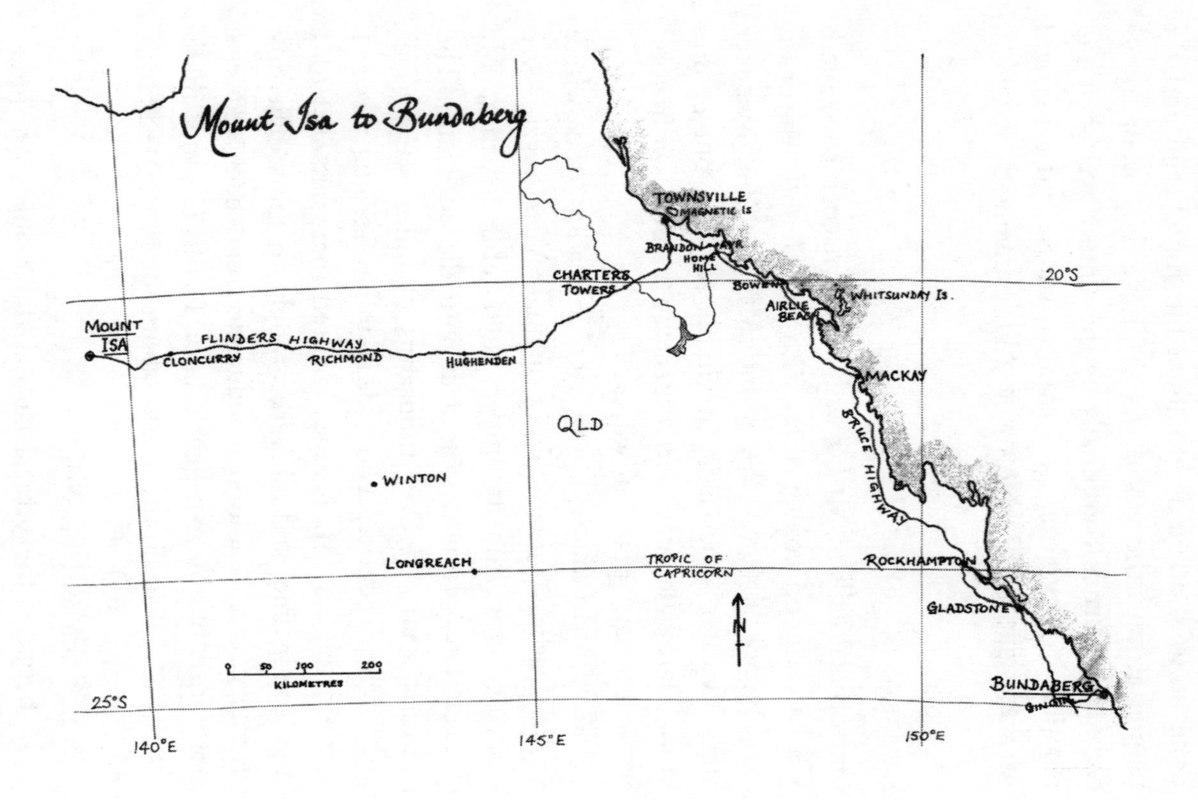
Mount Isa to Bundaberg
MOUNT ISA
FLINDERS HIGHWAY
CLONCURRY
RICHMOND
HUGHENDEN
CHARTERS TOWERS
TOWNSVILLE
MAGNETIC Is
BRANDON
AYR
HOME HILL
BOWEN
AIRLIE BEACH
WHITSUNDAY Is.
MACKAY
BRUCE HIGHWAY
QLD
WINTON
LONGREACH
TROPIC OF CAPRICORN
ROCKHAMPTON
GLADSTONE
BUNDABERG
N
0 50 100 200
KILOMETRES
20°S
25°S
140°E
145°E
150°E

President Digger James, whom we much admire, but almost forgot this was our 35th wedding anniversary (for which I had bought Hilary a pearl pendant in Darwin), until our elder son John telephoned from the UK. Naturally, we also discussed Diana's death. John told us of the growing mountains of flowers outside Buckingham and Kensington Palaces, and of the shock and anger in the UK.

Steve Hiscock returned to Brisbane next morning, leaving even before we enjoyed the fine dawn in the nearby hills as we drove off eastwards. The pale gold and green folded landscape was marred here and there by pylons. We recalled our younger son Charles's childhood view that there were two sorts of pylons, male and female, easily observable and recognisable, largely although not entirely by the 'clothes' they were 'wearing'. (Try it.) We sorted these pylons by sexes against the early morning big red sun and pink speckled clouds. We drove on to Cloncurry. The Cloncurry River still had water in parts. We drove the length of the Flinders Highway. The Black Plains are well named. The soil has no red in it at all. We thought Charters Towers a handsome town. I did more interviews by satellite telephone as we travelled.

After a rare shower of rain, we arrived in Townsville, Hilary driving. There, I did five more interviews about the death of the Princess of Wales and worked by fax and telephone. I left Mayor Tony Mooney, who had been most friendly and helpful over the years, a farewell letter: he was away at a local government conference in Cairns. I reflected, as I always did in Townsville, that it was here in 1995, in a speech at the close of Australia Remembers, that Paul Keating said the right things about the British role in Singapore in World War II (that photographic exhibition mentioned in chapter 1 had helped).

We took a few hours off to visit Magnetic Island, which we had long wanted to do, if only because of the erratic performance of Captain Cook's compass as he sailed past. As a sharp contrast to the Rolls, it was interesting and amusing to drive the Mini Moke we hired for a quick tour of Magnetic Island.

There was mist in the folds of the hills as we drove south-east from Townsville on the heavy humid morning of Day 25. A few kilometres from Townsville, a large truck was on its side off the road. This was the first accident we had seen in 13 800 km. Soon after came the first Queensland mango orchards, tulip trees, poinsettia bushes, water-lilies and sugarcane. A recently ploughed field was full of feeding magpie-geese. We saw a train bearing bulk molasses, and a second truck which had evidently taken a bend too speedily and turned right over. That day, driving through populated areas, there was much recognition of us and the Rolls, and much positive comment in restaurants, petrol stations and motels. As we drove through Brandon, road-workers waved. As we crossed the Burdekin River at Home Hill, people waved. And many drivers waved as we passed. All that probably had as much to do with sharing the grief at Diana's death as it did with RolleroundOz and its positive publicity.

We drove to Airlie Beach for a rare coffee stop. This is a lovely spot with its palms, yachts and, just across the warm blue water, the Whitsundays. One of my unfulfilled ambitions in Australia was a yachting holiday in these islands. We had dropped in near here for lunch during our illuminating and educational light aeroplane tour of far north Queensland with pilots John and Bill. Bill, a Queenslander, was the owner of the aircraft and could not resist joining us on that tour to see, for example, Cape York Peninsula and the mines and other places of British involvement or interest, including Charleville, Longreach, Mt Isa, Century Zinc, Weipa, RAAF Shergar, Aboriginal and Torres Strait Islander communities and the islands. Commercial diplomatic work apart, we found children at school on Yorke Island in touch by Internet with school-children in Cornwall. Pilot John Eglen, a former Brit, and Royal Navy officer, had much earlier broken his back and other things in a water-skiing accident when he hit a sub-merged log at speed. But he had recovered and returned to flying, and was a qualified and able instructor. He allowed me to take the controls for an hour or so as we flew south, including over the Whitsundays. Another Australian memory to treasure.

Shortly after our arrival in Mackay at the hotel where I had earlier stayed with a British Mining Trade Mission, I was invited to speak at an inter-denominational memor-ial service for Diana, Princess of Wales, early that evening in Mackay's Entertainment Centre. The Mayor, Councillor Julie Boyd, who had also been at the conference in Cairns, arrived in time to take part. The service was a straight-forward yet moving one, with some lovely music. By their account, it helped many of those there. Murray drove us there, and attended the service. He sat at the back and told us later he had estimated that between 1100 and 1200 people were present. I thought that an extraordinary turn-out at 5.30 pm on a working day in a busy town.

Next morning, we thought we had our first and only problem with the Rolls. The boot lock, which works both mechanically and electrically, seemed to fail. Murray and I made a jury-rig as a fall-back measure with, appropriately enough, red tape. But the lock worked perfectly well thereafter, and a later professional check found it faultless. Oh, we of little faith.

South of Mackay there were more sugarcane fields and some harvesting. This looked more mechanised and efficient than I recalled from Cuba or even Barbados or Mauritius—of which we were a little reminded by distant hills and the cane in the foreground. Sugar mill chimneys emitted plumes of white smoke. A very old double-decker bus, long ago converted into a campervan and once painted white, stood on the verge of the road displaying a sign 'Must Sell'. We saw why; but we wondered what particular kind of enthusiast would want to buy it.

For a while, the road was lined with lovely pink and white flowering bushes. We thought they might be related to oleander. Pineapples were now growing among the cane. An orchard of mini-orange trees was laden with fruit. The trees looked like ornamental ones. Brahmins and their soft-coloured new calves gleamed in the morning light. A bright array of red and cream poinsettias proudly announced a sugar mill entrance. Militarily groomed Norfolk pines mingled with ancient gums, scruffy she-oaks, ponderous pandanus palms, massive mangoes, flame of the forest with full seed pods ready to pop, ornamental oranges and brilliant bougainvilleas: the Queenslanders have a point about their lifestyle. The sight of the mangoes recalled both the finest we had ever tasted, in the Ord Valley, and the two huge mango trees in our garden in Jakarta. If we could save the fruit there from blind marauding fruit-bats with built-in radars, I would take full boxes to the Embassy in the boot of the official car, another pride of Britain—a Jaguar.

We suddenly drove into fog, but through it saw a mob of kangaroos eating in a fenced field, and cows drinking from a lily-covered pond. Later, before we stopped briefly in Gladstone, we admired an ironbark eucalyptus forest.

It seemed right that we had not seen a road train in Queensland, a home of railways. We had much enjoyed inspecting in Townsville the ex-London bus Gardiner-engined 'special' for the Normanton–Croydon run. We had also been shown the first-rate product of an Australia–UK joint venture, the luxury Edwardian-style coaches built for a Simplon-Orient quality ride from Townsville to Brisbane and eventually to Sydney and then west, perhaps all the way. I had much enjoyed discussing railways with the Mayor of Mackay. During RolleroundOz, I had a thoughtful letter from that other serious railway expert, Deputy Prime Minister Tim Fischer, thoughtfully suggesting an alternative route for us through Queensland. This was via Mt Isa, Winton, Longreach, Roma and Toowoomba, and it covered two railway routes. It looked excellent, but we had been to Longreach before, and more importantly, had obligations in Townsville, Mackay and Bundaberg, and had regretfully to decline Tim Fischer's suggestion.

•

And so to Bundaberg. We had long wished to visit there. Bundaberg sugar and rum is UK-owned, by Tate and Lyle. It is a productive and job-creating modern investment. We were tutored and guided ably in Bundaberg by Rod and Jenny Young. We covered the ground, from cane planting to sugar and its export, and to rum production. Morning tea with the Port Operations Manager and his wife Gillian in the port office was a treat. At the quayside nearby, a Greek ship was about to load 20 000 tonnes of sugar for Malaysia. We saw the mountains of sugar waiting to be loaded, in clearly a very efficient operation. We rode in a cane-harvesting machine as it cut several rows. Its operator, Paul, was welcoming and helpful. It was good to learn from someone who so evidently enjoyed his job. We visited energetic, inventive, amusing octogenarian sugar farmer Ned Churchward and his farm and house. Ned was pursuing exciting research on density of planting and trickle irrigation, which might well make a real difference to cane farming practices. He gave me some copies of key documents on his research for study in the UK: it might be useful for other crops. A generous act. And Ned and his wife Florrie showed us some fine examples of English stained glass in his house. We suggested they contact the Victoria and Albert Museum in London to learn more about them, as they were keen to do.

Buffet lunch was with a couple of dozen positive and cheerful members of the sugar farming community. Their positiveness was probably repeated throughout the community, I thought. We discussed the pros and cons of a tariff on sugar imports in the light of the then recent policy change on motor vehicles; the debate about whether to decelerate the reductions in the protective tariffs on textiles, clothing and footwear; and the National Farmers' Federation's pitch for a protective tariff for sugar. As in the UK, farmers here take a long view. And these farmers well knew they had a competitive edge in the world market. Given the pervasive uncertainties of the elements and the historical sense of farming for successive generations, that long view was entirely understandable. It was also admirable.

The sugar factory was a thrum of noisy production. Quality and technical checks were impressive. It was a surprise to see how easily the system could vary and switch among the variety of sugar types and products. This was market forces working well. The factory was also a lesson in mechanical engineering history. A venerable steam engine with a huge fly-wheel was still working smoothly and economically alongside its diesel motor descendants. It was a point of pride to the engineer that the steam engine should work so well and shine so brightly. I fancied the factory cat was also fond of the steam engine. She too was something of an institution. She enjoyed its warmth on a rare cold winter's night shift, and she had enjoyed its company through generations of electric diesels. She was of course deaf as well as old, but she understood every word of the engineer's, and some of ours.

This was another memorable day. We shall always be grateful to Rod and Jenny Young for showing us Bundaberg so thoroughly. They are justly proud of the company, and of the community.

That evening we had dinner in our motel room. In common with so many people around so much of the

Some Trade Issues

Australia is one of the leading five investors in the UK, above Japan. The UK is second only to the USA as an investor in Australia. Two-way trade and investment is large, lively and growing. Trade policy discussions between the UK and Australia are therefore positive and forward-looking, although there is the occasional problem such as over out-dated remaining protective State preferences. There are, too, some Australian–European Union trade discussions, such as those over veterinary matters, where the European Commission speaks on instructions and on behalf of EU Member countries. These can involve technical difficulties, and the occasional problem of principle, for example when a proposed bilateral agreement seemed to Australia to impinge unjustifiably on non-trade issues. Some Australians still feel they were not treated as well as they should have been when Britain joined the European Community, although the Australian economy seems to have done pretty well since that time. And European Union (mostly British) investment in Australia is huge and productive.

world, we watched the funeral of the Princess of Wales on television. It was an interesting mixture of British ceremonial (organised well in a short time), modern tributes and emotion. I was glad Australian Foreign Minister Alexander Downer and his wife Nicky were present. I also felt that the funeral was not the occasion for accusatory speeches, but that the ceremonial and the expressions of grief were necessary, justified and helpful. Our younger son rang to say that London had been almost silent all week.

This was not the end of an era. Diana died too young for that. But this dreadful death will surely bring changes for the better, notably in publicity media practices.

Bundaberg to Canberra 8

Unusually, Hilary drove first on Day 28, en route for Brisbane. Road trains were now well off the agenda, if never to be forgotten. We saw railway trains and cane trains a-plenty, some moving faster than the slow traffic on the roads. It was something of a shock to us to be driving on busy roads again, and to have our speed determined by traffic conditions rather than by speed limits, quality of road or our own wishes. The press of traffic was in great contrast to the north-west of the same State, and only partly because this was Father's Day.

The countryside, mostly dominated by sugarcane, also displayed elegant glades of tall eucalyptus, and artistic splashes of pink and white bauhinia trees. There were tropical fruit orchards. There were dams with lilies. And there was a paddock of sunflowers. They were past their prime, but still stood to attention, all heads towards the sun. Some 25 km north of Gympie we enjoyed a large

Bundaberg to Sydney
BUNDABERG
150°E
25°S
155°E
GYMPIE
CALOUNDRA
BRISBANE
QUEENSLAND
DUNDEE
GLEN INNES
NEW SOUTH
WALES
30°S
ARMIDALE
TAMWORTH
PORT
MACQUARIE
N
MUSWELLBROOK
NEWCASTLE
SYDNEY
0
50
100
200
KILOMETRES

vista of hills rolling into the distance. The land was so much greener and more fertile now.

The smartness of the smaller towns betokened civic pride. Larger Gympie looked prosperous, and was noticeably well supplied with sporting facilities, that essential prerequisite of one of Queensland's constant accomplishments and justified sources of pride, sporting success. Despite strong and well-argued bids from elsewhere, including Canberra with its Australian Institute of Sport resources and other attractions, the British Olympic team decided to do their pre-Sydney 2000 training in Queensland, at Griffith University.

Some 120 km north of Brisbane is a fine forest of tall gums. Hereabouts there are old Queenslander houses, looking cool and elegant. We diverted briefly to Caloundra. It would be interesting to compare the Coral Coast at Bundaberg with the Sunshine Coast here. And we could surely find some fish for lunch. There is a considerable physical difference between the two coastlines, and tourism is much more developed on the Sunshine Coast. We found fish and chips, and ate them on the beach, watching a family fishing on the end of a small jetty. The youngest boy of the family, in conversation with Hilary, confessed he really didn't like fishing at all. It was too boring. But he knew he had to pretend to enjoy it, for the sake of his father—and especially on Father's Day. Another holidaying family exercised their dog by lying on the jetty and from time to time throwing a ball into the water for the dog to retrieve, tirelessly.

We recalled that Sir Patrick (now Lord) Mayhew's stepmother lives near here. She had come to stay with us

Australian Sport

I grew up thinking that sport mattered in Britain, and have found it matters in varying degrees around the world, but nowhere more so than in Australia, where every politician has to have—and nearly always much enjoys—a sporting affiliation. This is partly due to the climate and the outdoor way of life. It is also, crucially, due to the enviable Federal and State investment and organisation. Expenditure on sport by the taxpayer has broad popular support, and when Sydney secured the 2000 Olympics, all Australia cheered—even Melburnians, who, after all, were hosts to the Olympics in 1956. (I recall the 1948 Olympics in England as a post-war and consequently fairly austere, but highly successful exercise in internationalism and endeavour. It must be the UK's turn again soon!)

in Canberra when her stepson, then Secretary of State for Northern Ireland (and our local MP), also stayed with us during an official visit.

We drove on south through the northern suburbs of Brisbane into the State capital. It was pleasant to relax at the Consul-General's Residence in Kenwood with Steve and Dee Hiscock and their children, and to catch up on some work.

Next day, the Rolls enjoyed only the third, and the last service check of the tour, at Austral Motors. We paid interesting farewell calls in this politically exciting State. Premier Rob Borbidge was away; but I had seen him a little earlier, and we exchanged letters. We paid calls on old friends Lord Mayor Jim Soorley, Chief Justice Macrossan and Deputy Opposition Leader Jim Elder, who had recently paid an official visit to the UK. We called also at Government House on the new Governor Major-General Peter Arnison and his wife Barbara, whom we had met briefly in another capacity, and who clearly had settled into their new role with alacrity and effectiveness. New to me also was the Speaker. After quite a fierce political battle, Jim Fouras had been succeeded by Neil Turner.

The calls were positive, friendly and useful. After the courtesies and business, Speaker Neil Turner treated us, as I am sure he does all his official callers, to a cracking display of skill with the bull-whip. Steve, Hilary and I feared for the chandelier and the coffee cups, but Neil's skill, rather than the risks we assumed he took, explained that fear. He shaved everything so close. To crack a long whip in an office both before and behind you, and narrowly to miss people, cups and State papers on the desk is, to say the least, a rare achievement. I wondered if Neil were ever tempted into taking his bull-whip with him into the Chamber when expecting a rowdy session.

As we drove away from Government House, down the sloping drive and through the fine gardens, Hilary and I recalled staying there with the Arnisons' predecessors, Governor Leneen Forde and her husband Angus. Leneen Forde was an inveterate traveller around her State. Born in Canada, and still possessed of an attractive Canadian accent, she had captured the hearts and loyalty of Queenslanders. I had no doubt the Arnisons would do the same. Angus, an ex-Queensland policeman, formed the DT Club (after Denis Thatcher), recruited a good membership for this exclusive club with its single, unstated, but obvious qualification for membership, and altogether enjoyed his time in Government House. He told me how he received so many club ties on official occasions that he had the Government House butler label each so that he could identify and wear them at the appropriate times. This was a good and sensible policy, in tie-conscious Australia.

We attended a business seminar held by the Queensland Chapter of the Australia–Britain Chamber of Commerce, and I spoke at the lunch. Rod Young of Bundaberg runs this modern and new Chapter inventively, meeting real commercial needs and doing much good.

That evening, the Hiscocks gave a happy and successful dinner by the pool for Consulate-General staff and British military exchange officers. There are over 70 members of the British Armed Services serving in Australia, doing operational jobs, and the same number of Australians serving with the British Forces. I recalled one British Army officer who, in his spare time, played rugby for the Australian Army team. Now there's international co-operation!

As I reported later to the *Canberra Times*, my tongue firmly in my cheek at the time, the evening of that dinner was unusually instructive. I did not explain why. The explanation follows now. Relaxing at midnight after the party, I went into our suite at the far end of the house and one storey up from where the party had been held. I wanted to check something we were discussing by reference to notes in my briefcase. In the suite, I discovered that we had been comprehensively burgled.

We travelled with small bags, for convenience overnight and for ease of access in the boot of the Rolls. The six most important and valuable bags had gone. In them, the burglars had taken cash for RolleroundOz and for ourselves, and some sterling we kept, as always, in case of a sudden need to fly to the UK; credit cards and, in a separate bag in an address book, a random list of unidentified PIN numbers; Hilary's vanity bag containing her best pieces of jewellery (for the formal occasions), including the new wedding anniversary pearl pendant; video and still cameras—together with all those excellent video tapes and undeveloped still film of all those marvellous RolleroundOz scenes and activities; passports, ID cards, a dictating machine, favourite Mont Blanc and Sheaffer pens, wallets, etc., etc.

Steve called the police. We telephoned Canberra and London to cancel credit cards. The police came quickly. Eventually, nine police officers were in the house. They did their best. We all searched the grounds. The police found Hilary's empty vanity bag, two others, our diplomatic passports and some items worthless to the burglars, including the meticulous financial accounts Hilary had kept of RolleroundOz, all sodden by overnight irrigation sprays. We made long lists for the police. They wrote reports and gave us reference numbers for insurance purposes. It was difficult to think of every item we had lost. It was easy to feel violated; and very disappointed. We supposed that we had provided a well-publicised target of opportunity, and that the chatter of the party around the pool, up from which the land sloped to the second storey, had provided good noise cover to help the burglars to effect a fairly easy entry. But our strongest feeling was that of relief: the Hiscock children, sleeping in rooms along the corridor on the same floor, had been undisturbed. And no one had been hurt.

At about 3.00 am the doorbell rang. I was close, and opened the door. Two policemen stood behind the door as I opened it. A young man, a reporter, stood before me and said, 'I understand you have been burgled.' For once thinking fast (plenty of adrenalin had flowed), I asked, accusingly and sternly, 'Have you been listening to the police radio?' (In the UK to do so is illegal, I understand.) His answer made it clear that he had. I continued that we had indeed been burgled; that that was all I was going to tell him; that there was no story; and that I'd be grateful if he reported nothing. To my surprise, he agreed; and said he was the only one who knew.

To my relief and real gratitude, he kept his word. Had the facts become generally known at the time, the burglary would have made the one dominating story of our farewell tour of Australia. RolleroundOz would not have been that rare phenomenon which the Australian press, radio and television people had been good enough both to discern and to create: a positive news story. The impact for the UK and the bonus for Australia–UK relations would have been lost.

The Queensland police went on doing their best the next morning. As the senior policeman responsible for diplomatic protection had predicted, more of the bags, bereft of valuables, were found. An off-duty policeman on his early morning cycle ride found Hilary's handbag and my briefcase by a creek. They had been emptied of anything of any use to the burglars. Some cards and letters were scattered around and in the creek. So were empty wallets, and our driving licences. I was relieved at that, since it lessened the consequential paper work. But I had been more relieved by the finding of our diplomatic passports the night before: I did not fancy explaining the need for new passports to the head of my own Consular Section in Canberra!

Evidently the burglary was a professional job. A white cotton glove, not ours, had been found by the creek, with the briefcase and handbag. The fingerprint experts found no trace of any print in or near the suite. Entry had been made with minimum effort and no fuss. The police believed that a gold brooch in the shape of an African elephant's head with white gold tusks and a diamond eye, which I had given Hilary two years before to celebrate my knighthood, would have been melted down in hours. The burglars had worked quickly, and with real luck with the separately recorded PIN numbers, removing twice the daily limit from our account by using the card both before and immediately after midnight, just before we cancelled the cards. Smart work.

One has simply, and mentally, to write off material loss, and this we did determinedly. After morning sessions with the attentive Queensland police, we drove down the Cunningham and New England Highways to Armidale, where we had a quiet dinner and stayed overnight. The countryside was attractive, including in Main Range National Park, where hundreds of bellbirds tolled as we climbed the pass. But much of this region, including the Darling Downs, was sadly dry. Below the Downs were a few small bright green patches of irrigated land. The New England names were a delight. I had never thought to see Ebbw Vale and Dundee within four hours' drive, even by Rolls-Royce. The grandeur of the McPherson Range to the left, and later of the Great Dividing Range either side of Glen Innes, helped to restore our spirits.

Next morning was noticeably cooler, as we continued south to Sydney through wooded hills dappled in the morning sunlight, and through gradually greening country. We began to see wattles again. By contrast, and recalling Day 1 as we had driven out of the Australian Capital Territory, billboards had appeared again in the outskirts of towns the moment we crossed the State border into New South Wales.

We shall remember the stretch from Armidale to Tamworth for a dead grey limb of a tree, leaning against a large lumpy rock and looking just like a giant goanna trying to secure a foothold; for two multicoloured parrots who diced with death by Rolls-Royce; and for the lovely views of the Moonbi Hills above Tamworth, wattles everywhere, gilding the scene.

We descended steeply into the valley of the River Peel and to Tamworth, whose outskirts were dominated by large agricultural machinery businesses and their warehouses. We learned by reference to the maps, guide books and a giant golden guitar at the roadside, that Tamworth is declaredly the country music capital—of Australasia. I wondered if that claim had been cleared with the Kiwis. Just south of Tamworth is the Aviation School owned by British Aerospace Australia. Further on, equestrian country dominated. Handsome stud farms, handsomely fenced, abounded. A farm dam was surrounded by horses. Three horses, their leading reins attached to the rear of a moving car, were being exercised smartly. And three white horses stood decorously in a glade of ghost gums.

As we approached the Hunter Valley, the first grapes we saw growing were near Muswellbrook. On the north side of Muswellbrook was an uncomplicated and telling Vietnam War Memorial. We enjoyed the Hunter region again, recalling our 1995 underground coalmine visit, and our visit that same year with the then Lord Mayor of London, including to the Calais Winery. The 1993 Reserve Shiraz and Cabernet Sauvignon I bought then drank well in 1997. We were sorry there was not time for a diversion via Newcastle where we had had some particularly good times, professional and personal, and where British Aerospace were to provide some good new jobs. As we progressed southwards towards Sydney, power stations loomed, and pylons (male and female again) marched towards the coast and the metropolis. The increasing industrialisation was a distinct and almost jarring change from all the varied scenery we had seen. On Day 31 of RolleroundOz, Sydney itself was a claustrophobic contrast to the expansive emptiness of so much of the Australia we had driven through and enjoyed so deeply. But Sydney, as ever, was also a joy to enter.

We stayed two nights in Sydney, in our necessary and convenient official Vaucluse pied-à-terre, which used to be part of the large Residence for the Consul-General. In the 1980s and earlier, the High Commissioner had used a flat kept for him in Point Piper. I had known the flat, its dining room and its superb view from a visit in the 1980s. I had also known its cost; and since then the Public

Accounts Committee in London had had their cost-conscious way. Point Piper or Vaucluse, the saving in hotel expenses is enormous.

We spent the first of our two evenings in Sydney at a celebratory dinner at the Observatory Hotel generously given by Stephen Timperley and his wife. Stephen is Managing Director of Fox, Rolls-Royce & Bentley. The able Stephen had been in Sydney only a few months. He was unfailingly positive and helpful about RolleroundOz. It was a delight to meet at his dinner some of New South Wales's heavy-hitting Rolls-Royce and Bentley owners; and fun to tell them a few RolleroundOz stories. The first official call in Sydney was on Speaker Hon. John Murray. I slightly overstayed my warm welcome and was therefore a little late for good friend Hon. Max Willis, President of the Legislative Council. Among other kindnesses, Max had opened in Sydney, with me and in the presence also of Margaret Thatcher, that photographic exhibition on the UK's role in World War II in the Far East and the Pacific. It was always an amusing and educational experience to talk with Max. I paid an interesting and pleasant call too on Leader of the Opposition (and Naval Reserve Officer) Peter Collins QC, whom I had also come to know quite well. I had greatly enjoyed a number of discussions on matters economic and financial with Governor of the Reserve Bank Ian MacFarlane, and was very glad to be able to call on him too, for another helpful session.

The NSW Governor was away. We would, however, return twice more to Sydney, after RolleroundOz. Once would be to accompany a British Minister of State at the

Foreign and Commonwealth Office, Derek Fatchett, and to pay a farewell call on Premier Bob Carr. That meeting was interrupted by a press call when Bob Carr handed over to Derek Fatchett books of the condolence pages written and signed at New South Wales government offices on the death of Diana, Princess of Wales. Some had written moving tributes. Some had simply signed. There were, in all, some 15 000 pages.

Our second and last visit to Sydney while I was High Commissioner was on our way home to England from Canberra after mandatory retirement from the British Civil Service at 60. We travelled home by way of an evening and night in Sydney, a month's holiday in the South Island of New Zealand and a voyage thence in a container ship around Cape Horn to arrive in Tilbury Docks, London, just in time for Christmas. That warm October evening in Sydney, we dined in Cammeray above Middle Bay at the house of good friends we had first met in Indonesia. Colin McLachlan, a senior Sydney businessman, had demonstrated and enhanced this friendship by allowing me to sail the yacht he kept just below his house. And Phillippa and he gave us a marvellous dinner on our last night in Australia, complete with mutual friends Jean and John Coplin who, travelling from the UK to Indonesia, had diverted to Sydney for the occasion.

Lunch on the day of official calls in Sydney was given in the Consulate-General offices overlooking the harbour and bridge by Consul-General Philip Morrice, who kindly invited some splendid Sydney men of Academe, business and the Australia–Britain Society—men I had known, worked with and admired. It was a most memorable farewell occasion.

After lunch, I had a meeting with my opposite number, the Australian High Commissioner in London, Hon. Dr Neal Blewett, who was then visiting Sydney. As always with Neal, this was a pleasant, professional and profitable meeting. There was also a press call at Fox, Rolls-Royce & Bentley—and Murray returned the unused kit of spares. I returned to Vaucluse for some work. In the evening, Hilary and I had a thoroughly entertaining and stimulating dinner with good friends Annabel and Ken Baxter, two more very fine Australians.

Sydney's top businessmen, like Melbourne's, are enormously rewarding to know. It goes without saying that they are world-class. I had found it thoroughly stimulating to work with some of them. Ken Baxter, formerly a very senior government official, quickly established equal eminence in the business field. Distinctly successful lawyer, businessman and shrewd investor John Landerer CBE is also a man of genuine and successful charitable endeavour. He does good by stealth, including the promotion of Anglo–Australian relations. Among many possible examples, I found it testing and enjoyable to negotiate with Ken Cowley, when he ran the newspaper the *Australian*, over a supplement to be devoted solely to *new*IMAGES. I particularly enjoyed one exchange with him when I had finally tracked him down: this was by telephone, I in my office, and he in his aeroplane on the way to Hong Kong. I found Ted Harris, inter alia Chairman of British Aerospace Australia, a source of wise advice and much co-operation and friendship. However, I confess, the most amusing Australian businessman I met, and one who also much impressed me with his skill, success and philanthropy, was Lindsay Fox of Melbourne —now also of Fox, Rolls-Royce & Bentley of Sydney!

The British Council's operations in Australia are based in Sydney. The year of *new*IMAGES, 1997, was also the 50th anniversary of the Council in Australia. The Council's operations are conducted most thoughtfully and effectively under its fine Director, Jim Potts. Jim put heart, soul and his considerable erudition into the cultural, scientific and educational side of *new*IMAGES and led a wonderful team. He and my first Deputy, David Fall (now British Ambassador in Hanoi), and later Andrew Pocock formed the Project Board for *new*IMAGES, and did excellent work. Jim's exceptional service was recognised in the 1998 New Year's Honours with an OBE. Jim also made a notable contribution to RolleroundOz by arranging for me to have copies of *Literary Links*, an astute and enjoyable collation of Australian and British writings, then just published, to present to some of the senior people on whom we called around Australia. That book is an enduring and tangible memory, recalling not only Sydney, not only the exhibition which preceded and led to *Literary Links*, but also the author, Roslyn Russell, and Brisbane, where we had dinner and a very good conversation with her.

•

Sydney has always thrilled us. I first saw it in 1983. Like so many visitors and Sydney-siders, I will always carry the imprint of the view from the port side of an aeroplane landing from the north. The many associations with Captain Cook and the First Fleet; that harbour Governor Phillip described so aptly; the development and growth of Sydney with British backing; the view from Vaucluse of the central business district skyscrapers at dawn, the low sun transforming them into lozenge-cut jewels; Sydney Opera House, its architectural history and the brilliance of the best of its productions; sailing from the harbour out through the Heads, and sailing in through the Heads; Sydney's restaurants; Sydney's older and youngest architecture; Sydney's parliament and politics; Sydney Cricket Ground; Sydney's northern suburbs and southern bays; Sydney's business enterprise and spirit of innovation and endeavour; and, above all, Sydney's people will be among our treasured memories.

Sydney is indeed a cosmopolitan town so different from Melbourne—a little self-conscious, perhaps, but proudly and justly so. Seen from Sydney, it is Melbourne that is so far out of town. In this centre of sporting achievement and of action as well as activity, Sydney 2000 should genuinely be the best Olympics ever. I worry, a little, only about transporting so many people to so many events, and the difficulty in justifying huge investments for a few weeks' colossal load on the transport system, but Sydney will show I am wrong to worry at all. And talented, thrilling, friendly Sydney will, we hope, let us return—often.

•

Day 33, the last of RolleroundOz, began with that particularly attractive drive around the bays into downtown Sydney. Breakfast was the first engagement. It was with President of the Australia–Britain Chamber of Commerce Phil Higginson, Secretary Jacqi Cross and Director of Trade Promotion (and Deputy Consul-General) Peter Spiceley. Next came a business call with First Secretary Defence Equipment David Richardson (also a recent OBE) on Jean-Georges Malcor and his staff at the impressive Anglo–French joint venture Thompson-Marconi Sonar. A good and valuable start to the day.

An unusual addition to the original plan followed. After checking that the Patron, HE Governor-General Sir William Deane, approved, I had accepted an invitation from the Aids Trust of Australia to launch in Sydney the Diana, Princess of Wales HIV/AIDS Appeal. It was easy to write a speech for such a purpose, and a pleasure as well as a memorable exercise in trying to help those doing good, in meeting people who manifestly do good all the time, and in being associated with just one of no doubt very many appropriate memorials to Diana, Princess of Wales.

•

Then hotfoot the short way to Canberra. There was no hope of driving down the coast to Batemans Bay and back home through Braidwood and Bungendore. There was time only for a quick last lunch in our favourite Village Tea Room in Berrima. I could not be late for the last appointment on RolleroundOz, a 5.00 pm farewell call on

Bundaberg to Canberra

Kate Carnell, Chief Minister of the Australian Capital Territory. Kate had become another friend. We much admire her single-minded devotion to duty and the ACT, her growth in the job and her consequently large personal following which defies local political history. And Kate was a good friend of the British High Commission. She would often come to our events. She was particularly good in supporting and helping *new*IMAGES, including allowing Canberra's principal and prominent floral bed, on Civic

Hill, to be planted with flowers in the design of the *new*IMAGES logo, and then to 'open' it.

We had missed the local Canberra news and I therefore had no idea that Kate's head had very recently been shaved for a charity. I hope I passed the implicit test of diplomacy when I first greeted her! Kate certainly raised a great deal of money for a particularly good cause. That farewell call was a good one, if also a little sad. We had a good talk about Canberra and about Canberran and Federal politics. It was a right way to end RolleroundOz proper.

But we felt guilty of a serious sin of omission: we had not included Tasmania.

Tasmania, and Conclusions

9

We had tried to include Tasmania in RolleroundOz. In the High Commission, Vicki Baxter Amade had concluded, from conversation with Hobart, that some people in Tasmania were a little miffed at our failure. So, on return to Canberra, we tried again. These efforts too were frustrated, by a combination of the incidence of ferry times, other duties for which I needed the Rolls, and work requiring me to be in Canberra, Sydney and Adelaide. The need to visit Adelaide again was in connection with that murder in Saudi Arabia. The problems involving Australia in that tragic, complex and fraught affair were themselves difficult and at times tense; but they were resolved with goodwill and much effort by those concerned.

Tasmania, we had found, does genuinely feel 'left off the bottom'—even literally off maps from time to time. I suppose it is in part a reaction to this feeling, and to the jokes about Tasmania and Tasmanians (there is nearly

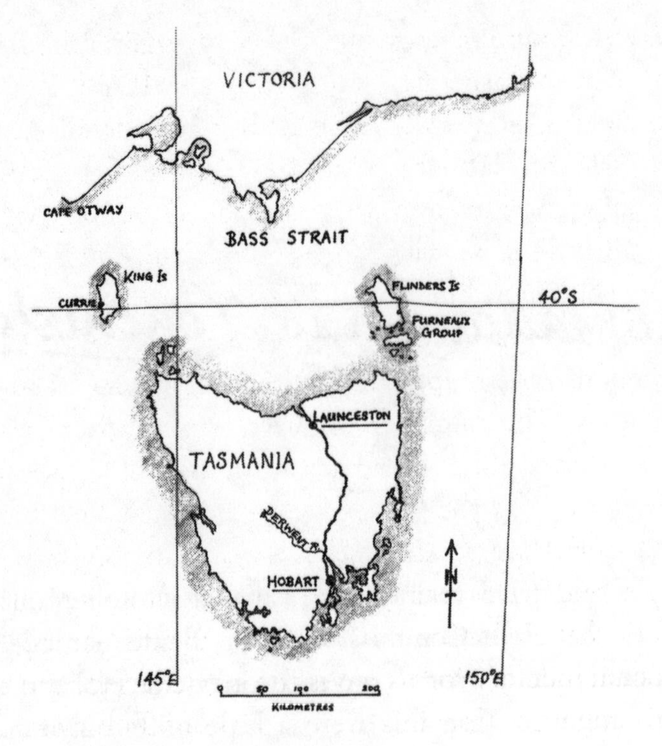

Hobart to Launceston

always one region of a country, or country in a region, of which derogatory jokes traditionally are told), that Tasmanians sometimes call the main body of Australia 'the North Island' in Tasmania. I particularly enjoyed King Island's own version, lying as it does between 'the North Island' and 'the South Island'.

Tasmania's economy tends to just hang on to the rest, despite much leadership and devoted effort by many, including politicians, officials and business people. But some of the State's broad range of resources offer good prospects. Sound investment is vital, naturally. One British investment in Tasmania, dating from the 1930s, but kept up to date, is the Cadbury chocolate factory in Claremont, a suburb of Hobart. Cadbury Schweppes recently designed, constructed and commissioned a chocolate factory in China. The whole project was run not from the United Kingdom, but from Claremont.

The 1996 massacre at Port Arthur, a favourite tourist destination, was an appalling blow to Tasmania, in so very many ways. The massacre followed shortly after another insane mass killing in Dunblane, Scotland. We were doubly moved by the horror in Port Arthur. We attended the memorial service there, with Governor Sir Guy and Lady Green. Descending in a helicopter with them towards that gathering of people in grief is an indelible Australian memory for us. So is the service itself, and talking to members of the bereaved families afterwards. Tasmania's beauty, so different from that of so much of Australia, in parts so reminiscent of some of the prettiest parts of Britain, had captured us early on. The beauty of the Hobart to Port Arthur area, seen from a helicopter, was part of that memorial service day for us, adding further poignancy to the grief. With all these memories and influences, we very much wanted to pay a proper personal farewell to the island, as well as to pay official respects, and to include Tasmania in RolleroundOz.

Eventually, we could get away for two days, so we flew to Hobart to stay at their invitation with the very hospitable Greens in glorious Government House. We greatly enjoy the company of Guy and Rosslyn, and had a splendid evening with them. We talked over dinner about

Antarctica, a particular interest of both Tasmania and Tasmania's very able Governor. We also discussed security in official Government Residences; climate change; Tasmania's economic development; the Derwent River; catamaran ferries built in Tasmania and exported first to the UK, where they now ply in summer between England and France, and in the Southern summer between the two islands of New Zealand; and all manner of interesting subjects—economic, political, social and historical.

Official farewell calls followed the usual pattern: on Speaker Dr Frank and Mrs Madill, Opposition Leader Jim Bacon and Premier Tony Rundle. We missed another of our favourite Tasmanians, former Mayor Doone, who had once received us bearing crutches, and clearly in pain. As usual there was some business to conduct, as well as the courtesies. And, as ever in Tasmania, there was a particularly hospitable welcome and a relaxed, enjoyable atmosphere. We also called, of course, on our splendidly effective Honorary British Consul in Tasmania, Paul Kemp, who runs the Trust Bank.

Paul is now Britain's only Honorary Consul in Australia. I have often considered the case for appointing one in Darwin, and that may be the right thing to do before too long. We shall be hard pressed anywhere to find someone as understanding, sensible and sound as Paul. There has to be mutual advantage in the appointment of Honorary Consuls. For example, the perceived status of the incumbent may be of some business advantage to him. The burden of work is usually not heavy, though it can at times be so on the Honorary Consul's assistant or secretary. While the fundamental duties, at a 'first-aid' level, are to help British subjects in difficulty, it is good also to have an Honorary Consul who has an interest in as well as an eye to trading opportunities.

It was, as always, a pleasure to call on Premier Tony Rundle. We did this in Launceston where he was then working. When, a little before the Port Arthur Memorial service, Tony Rundle led a delegation to other cities of Australia to explain that Port Arthur was safe again, and to encourage tourists to return, he and his party took an evening off to dine with us in Westminster House. He later paid a useful and successful official visit to the UK, including to Dunblane and Edinburgh.

The drive north from Hobart to Launceston on the Midland Highway was on a lovely day in late spring. We were reminded once again of parts of the west country of England, even of Wales. We regretted, as ever, not having enough time to visit more of the island, including the national parks. We recalled that over 20 per cent of Tasmania has been declared a World Heritage Area.

Tasmania has man-made attactions too. The handsome Tasman Bridge stands tall, strong and elegant across the Derwent, despite missing one of its many piers. An errant ship disposed of the pier—and most of a span with it—causing loss of life as cars fell into the river. We met the widow of the Briton responsible for the design and construction of this remarkably fine bridge in Norfolk Island, of all unlikely places. Sensibly, she had retired there. Further coincidences emerged in conversation over dinner with Mrs Reid. She and her late husband had lived in the small village in Wiltshire where (and when) Hilary and I were married. And they had shown film of their travels—and of bridges, of course—to some neighbours, including Hilary's parents.

It was in Tasmania that we first watched England play cricket in Australia. Like Sir Alec Douglas-Home, we were grateful for the rain, which probably prevented a very early England defeat in that, for England, not the happiest of Test tours in Australia. At the attractive Tasmanian cricket ground at Bellerive we met Denis Rogers, then in charge of cricket in Tasmania, later to lead so effectively at national level. Denis and his wife Lynn were such friendly people whom we were delighted to see at several airport lounges and cricket grounds around Australia, and at Lord's when the Australians toured England in 1997. Australia won that series too, but these things are cyclical, Denis, and England shall prevail again!

It was essential to include both the north and south of Tasmania in this farewell visit. The early history and growth of Tasmania as two separate colonies was accompanied by regional rivalry, which persists to this day. Thus, for example, two newspapers, and two campuses of the University of Tasmania (with, no doubt, much travel for senior staff between the two). On our first official visit to Tasmania, we had been only to Hobart: that this was a mistake became crystal clear. We arrived in Launceston that lovely spring day in time for a real treat—lunch with Sir Raymond and Lady Ferrall at the Launceston Club. They and their other guests were eloquent in answer to our questions about Launceston and Tasmanian life. Lunch was fun. We have enjoyed Launceston, and learned much, especially on our first visit there, which included a visit to the Mayor's Parlour. A cousin of my mother's,

Frank Jordan, was Mayor of the Cornish town of Launceston, from where I imagine the Tasmanian town took its name. Tasmanians pronounce all three syllables of Launceston. In England, the middle 'ces' is elided. (Some Cornish people drop the 't' and say 'Lahnson'.) I could not find an adequate explanation for this striking difference. Perhaps the Tasmanian pronunciation was 'corrected', either on adoption or by a successor generation.

Every time we visited Tasmania, we bought another piece of hand-crafted beauty in black-hearted sassafras. Tasmanian woods, from myrtle to tea tree, combine with Tasmanian wood-turning and Tasmanian design to make many unique and admirable pieces of art. We shall always enjoy ours. And a small log of Huon pine from Tasmania now rest in my workshop: it waits to be fashioned into another treasured reminder.

We were silent and a little sad as we flew back to Canberra from Launceston. Sad to leave this southern and in some special ways rather separate part of Australia. Sad to leave its different and often intense unspoiled beauty. Sad to have to say goodbye. And sad again, as ever, about the Port Arthur massacre. Before the massacre a visit to Port Arthur had been an essential thing to do, perhaps particularly for British people. The penal colony there had in some ways been a modern, even enlightened institution for its time, intended to promote reform through punishment. Initially, only those convicted of less serious crimes were sent to Port Arthur penitentiary. As Robert Hughes explains in *The Fatal Shore*, it was not as bad as Macquarie Harbour or Norfolk Island: it was 'conceived and run as a purgatorial grinding-mill rather than a torture chamber'. However, it had a terrible reputation as a place of misery. We saw there plain evidence of the stern conditions under which the convicts, guilty in many cases of rather petty crimes, worked off their heavy debt to society. We first saw the roofless penitentiary one evening deserted and in the rain; and we experienced the ghostly atmosphere of the place.

Although we were now sure that Port Arthur itself was newly dedicated to running an important tourist attraction in a place of haunting beauty, and that once again it was an essential place to visit, for us it would also be saddening indeed to return—to the ghosts of the massacre, to the site of the memorial service, and to that newly erected tall cross of Tasmanian woods, rough-hewn, simple, but impressive and indestructible, at which flowers were placed to commemorate those slaughtered innocents.

As we flew back, we thought too of the evening of the commemoration of the Battle of Britain, in Hobart in September 1996. We knew that Australians had played heroic parts in that vital battle, a turning point in World War II, and a testing time for the Royal Air Force and all Britain, a time when we needed friends, badly. We knew, however, that rather few of the gallant young men who had died in the Battle of Britain were Australian. We were deeply impressed, then, to find that the Battle was commemorated each year by a service at the Australian War Memorial in Canberra, complete with a Royal Australian Air Force flypast. It was evident that the commemoration was of the supreme sacrifice, of shared sacrifice in the defence of freedom, and of extraordinary heroism in air battle. In Hobart, every year, a dinner is organised to commemorate all of the above, together with the heroism and the sacrifice of Bomber Command, in which many Australians served, and in which large numbers died. That year, I was asked to go and speak at the dinner. That dinner is itself now a treasured Australian memory of ours. As I wrote the speech, I thought of living on the west side of London in war-time, spending many nights in an air-raid shelter, and watching battles in the air. We young boys could draw all the aeroplanes our heroes were flying, and we cheered them as they fought in the skies above us. As I wrote, and as I delivered the speech, I thought too of Hilary's father flying in Bomber Command during the war, and of my own father who had served with the RAF in Palestine between the wars, and who during World War II had worked on the production and servicing of Armed Forces vehicles during the day and on organising the local Home Guard at night.

Perhaps my most enduring memory of that commemorative evening in Hobart was listening to a former Battle of Britain pilot speak, from direct and certain knowledge.

The following morning I was one of a number, with the Governor, laying wreaths on the top of a hill in a southerly Tassie gale roaring up the Derwent River. The RAAF had arranged elastic bungy cords to prevent the wreaths from flying away. We had to prevent ourselves from being blown away. It was nonetheless a dignified ceremony which, like the evening before, inspired us all to think and to remember.

I suggested that the speaker at the dinner the following year should be another former Battle of Britain pilot, also living in Australia—a former Air Adviser at the

British High Commission, Air Commodore James Coward RAF Retd. James is in his eighties, and is an accomplished and inexhaustible raconteur. He flew Spitfires in the Battle of Britain. One summer's afternoon, he was shot out of his Spitfire and came floating down towards the Cambridgeshire village of Duxford on his war-time hemispherical silk parachute. Standing at the village church door below was a young bride-to-be, awaiting her groom, who had been held up no doubt by the air-raid warning. The bride, holding her bouquet, watched the young man suspended in mid-air tying a tourniquet around his shattered leg to try to stanch the flow of blood. James was also trying to prevent the leg from falling off. The parachute slowly disappeared from view beyond the village houses. The bridegroom eventually arrived. The two were married, and the bride sent her bouquet to the hospital for the young RAF flyer. James eventually came round from the inevitable coma. By his hospital bedside he saw his own young wife, Cynthia. If he was conscious of the flowers, then he assumed they were from his wife. James recovered; but with only one leg. He returned to the RAF but not, of course, to flying. He was sent to serve on the personal staff of Winston Churchill. Forty years later at a dinner in Australia, James was telling his modest version of part of this story. There was a pause. Then from the end of the table, a British-born lady, whom James did not know, quietly asked: 'Did you get my flowers?'

•

Tasmania, and Conclusions

James and Cynthia Coward are just two of over a million Brits-become-Australians, most of them dual nationals. Beyond this million, another 1.4 million Australians have a parent born in Britain. The UK remains a principal source of immigration into Australia. The Consular Section in the British High Commission in Canberra issues more British passports than any other such office outside the United Kingdom—some 62 000 in 1996. And the figure keeps growing. The Consular Section also provides Entry Certificates for Australian working holiday-makers in the UK—in the most generous such system anywhere in the world. The Consular Section does not issue visas to Australians, because Australians do not need visas to visit the UK for up to six months. The fact that Australia requires visas of British people (and everyone else) is the reason for long queues around Australia House in London and Australian consulates around Britain every year—although the new electronic travel authority will help.

The family ties between our two countries are enormous in number and scope. We have vital values in common: democracy; the rule of law; freedom of expression, of religion, of the press; human rights—and so on. Visible trade between us in 1997 was running at over $A27 billion (£13 billion) a year. Invisible two-way trade is worth at least as much. Both are growing healthily. So is investment each way. Australia vies with France and Germany to be the third largest external investor in the UK—and much of that investment is recent, modern. It amounted to over $A27 billion in 1997. The UK is by a close margin second to the USA as the largest external investor in Australia. As we left the country, British investments there were valued at over $A100 billion. Much of that investment too is recent. It creates and sustains jobs (somewhere between 270 000 and 300 000, we estimated), and contributes to the economy importantly and in ways that add high value. Investment from the USA was worth a few billion dollars more. Number three investor, Japan, was at a significantly lower figure, about $A57 billion.

Political co-operation on international matters between Britain and Australia covers the gamut of subjects of international debate and is, with very few exceptions, easy to do, worth doing, and valuable to others as well as to ourselves. The occasional disagreement on matters multinational is discussed from a basis of ready understanding of the other's position, of the largest range of assumptions in common I can recall from an entire diplomatic career, and without 'flannel'. Bilateral negotiation can be tough, even just occasionally rough, but the spirit is always straightforward, and resolution is achieved.

Defence co-operation between Britain and Australia surprised and pleased me in its depth, quality and usefulness to each of us. I mentioned Exchange Officers in chapter 8. I mentioned examples of naval co-operation in chapters 4 and 5. Co-operation between the two armies and air forces, in the UK, in Australia and in third countries, is also profound. The Integrated Air Defence System of the Five-Power Defence Arrangements is one of many examples. And those Scottish pipers and drummers I referred to in chapter 2 are also infantrymen, and when in Australia were also engaged in competitions and exercises. Exercise Longlook involves well over 100 servicemen and women simply exchanging jobs between

The Australian Military

Gallipoli, where the young Australian forces part of an Allied army were blooded—and badly bloodied, is seared into Australian consciousness. A feature film, shown annually, perhaps rather romanticises the military defeat and the mistakes of war, and seems to me wrongly to imply that British officers in command sacrificed Australian and New Zealand troops rather than British. But ANZAC Day commemorating the Gallipoli landings is observed throughout Australia, and genuine honour is justly paid to Australian military veterans. ANZAC Day is also commemorated in Westminster Abbey and elsewhere in the UK. Australia's record—in wars, conflicts and, for example in support of the UN, in peace—is striking and impressive. And Australia Remembers commemorating the 50th Anniversary year of the end of World War II, and drawing lessons, was an example to the world. The proud and professional Australian Armed Services retain close co-operative and productive links with Britain in intelligence, equipment and personnel exchanges, military exercises—including in the Five-Power Defence Arrangements—and policy discussion and implementation.

Australia and the UK for three months or so every other year. Intelligence cooperation and sharing is rightly unsung, but, again, it is deep. It runs the gamut from collection through assessment to use. Defence co-operation is sometimes linked with political co-operation on international matters: the military transport for the Australian medics doing such vital work in Rwanda was provided and run by the British Army.

I heard quite a bit in Australia about the disagreement between Prime Ministers Churchill and Curtin during World War II over the best deployment of Australian troops. I heard views about the Australian Defence Force's progress away from early dependence on Britain under Colonial and later Dominion status. I read the histories. I found them less coloured than the versions I had heard. I found the Churchill–Curtin exchanges of telegrams to be compelling and impressive reading. Each Prime Minister's extraordinarily detailed arguments are deployed in a thoroughly gentlemanly fashion: courteous, clear, straightforward. Although these two leaders disagreed in this instance, and were party political opponents, they clearly had real and deep respect for each other. I think historians would agree that the finest and most moving memorial service for Curtin was the one Churchill ordered to be held in London.

I have held the Churchill–Curtin relationship as a paradigm for the conduct of relations today between our two countries. For most of our time in Australia, there were governments in London and Australia of opposing political persuasions. John Howard was right to say in London in mid-1997, soon after Tony Blair became British Prime Minister, that in our respective regions no two countries know each other as well, trust each other more, or have closer relations. The reference to our respective regions may have been both a diplomatic politesse for others to hear, and a sensible qualification, but for Britain, in my own experience, it could be removed.

Tasmania, and Conclusions

All this co-operation, all the history (including of our educational systems), and all the shared values helped to explain why I found that in the conduct of government business between us, we and the Australians thought alike. We had both assumptions and thought processes in common. It was thus a matter of ease and pleasure to conduct business, even, almost always, on the rare occasions when we disagreed.

The view of some of the information media in both countries was different. They made different assumptions—for example, of antagonism because of personality or party; and they developed, sometimes, the most extraordinary stories. One of the false assumptions concerned me, because I found it adopted by some dedicated followers of some of the media in both countries. It was that the British Government believed that the status quo in Australia, the constitutional monarchy, ought not to change; and that to argue for its change was in some way to be anti-British. Nonsense. The British Government did indeed have a view about the Australian constitutional debate: that it was nothing to do with us. Australian cabinets understood that well. There was thus no problem between the British and the Australian governments on this subject. The media assumption, or assertion, was simply wrong, baseless.

It follows that I do not agree with those few who say that if and when Australia were to become a republic, relations between our two countries would improve. There is not all that much room for improvement, save in popular misperceptions at, as it were, the tabloid level of comment. The correct judgment, I believe, is that if

Australia were to make the constitutional change the republican movement there is pursuing, it would make no difference at all to the substance of our bilateral relations.

I sketch this background to Australia–UK relations because it was the background to my Federal farewell calls in Canberra. They are too many to list. I should record that the Governor-General and Lady Deane gave us the particular honour of a farewell luncheon at Government House. Prime Minister John Howard and Janette gave us a truly memorable farewell dinner at The Lodge with, also, the Deputy Prime Minister and Judy Fischer, ABC Chairman Donald McDonald and Janet, and the then Secretary for Foreign Affairs Philip and Carol Flood. (Carol and Philip were also colleagues and friends in Indonesia, and were recently, to our delight, appointed to London.) Jointly, the President of the Senate Hon. Margaret Reid and the then Speaker of the House of Representatives Hon. Bob Halverson gave us dinner in the President's Suite—another most enjoyable memory. Albeit necessarily in absentia, the Chief of the Defence Force John Baker, represented by the then Vice-Chief Chris Barrie, dined us out in fine style at Duntroon with the Secretary for Defence, the Service Chiefs, my Defence Adviser, and our wives. The Director of the Office of National Assessments, Richard Smith, gave me lunch with senior members of his staff and mine. The Australian Capital Territory Branch of the Australia–Britain Society laid on a fine and generous reception at the much admired Commonwealth Club. And we were treated to a farewell lunch in Parliament House by the Australia–UK Parliamentary Friendship Group, chaired by the distinguished Father of the House of Representatives—and now Speaker—the Rt. Hon. Ian Sinclair.

All this we deeply appreciated. All this reflected the background of extraordinarily close bilateral co-operation between two countries with many shared values, and with much shared history, but for many years now thoroughly independent of each other (partly due to Britain's early urging), and half a world apart.

On the diplomatic front, the doyen of the Diplomatic Corps, the Maltese High Commissioner George Busuttil, thoughtfully gives a small reception for each departing Head of Mission, with some of his or her closest colleagues. This is a sensible and welcome arrangement we had not met elsewhere, and is bereft of the normal polite artificiality that accompanies some diplomatic niceties and courtesies. We valued George's practice. We also valued highly a dinner given by our particular friends and diplomatic colleagues from two posts, the French Ambassador and his wife, Dominique and Maud Girard. Dominique and I were ambassadors together in Jakarta. I admired his professionalism and skill, and enjoyed his company there. I admired his professionalism in Canberra still more, during a thoroughly difficult period in Franco–Australian relations over French nuclear testing in the South Pacific. At the Girards' dinner, Foreign Minister Alexander Downer and Dominique spoke wittily, kindly and well.

Farewell calls in Canberra included those on the Prime Minister, most of his Cabinet and other ministers and parliamentary leaders. As ever, it was good to do some pieces of business with hard-working ministers and others, as well as the courtesies. I called too on some of the senior officials I had dealt with most, including the Secretary of the Department of the Prime Minister and Cabinet, the impressive and amusing Max Moore-Wilton.

It was a professional plus that during my last couple of weeks as High Commissioner, two British ministers from the new Labour Government came to Australia. These official visits helped further to boost *new*IMAGES, as well as to do useful work in the foreign affairs and defence fields.

•

During and as a result of RolleroundOz, we learned, understood, formed judgments about and enjoyed so much. We shall not forget the warm informality and genuine friendliness of outback dwellers. We shall not forget that, rather like other Scots, Aberdeen Angus thrive anywhere; that cricket is as religious a pursuit as any on the part of devotees throughout this vast continent of a country; that one of the highest temples of that religion is cricket against England; that *new*IMAGES both was needed and has had a clear positive impact; that our bilateral relationship, if not always fully and correctly understood, is valued, and mostly for the right reasons; that nonetheless there is plenty more to be done in managing and further developing and extending Australia–UK relations to mutual advantage; that Australia is a fine, stimulating country of extraordinary beauty and possessed of some great citizens—including world-citizens; that we should return and tour again, slowly, and probably by four-wheel drive; and yet that the finest way to see Australia is by Rolls-Royce.

The three and a quarter years Hilary and I spent in Australia amounted in many ways, personal and professional, to the time of our lives. It is always professionally stimulating for a diplomat to serve in a country during a change in the government of his own country; still more during a change in the government of the country to which he is accredited. I had both stimuli. There was the fun of closely following someone else's elections. There was the challenge of change in some policies and in some of the means of pursuing the business and interests of UK Ltd. And there was the challenge of change in dealing with different ministers, even if we had come to know many of the Australian Coalition Government ministers during their time in opposition.

I sought a farewell call on former Australian Prime Minister Paul Keating, in part as a courtesy, and in part for nostalgic reasons; but he came to Westminster House for the purpose. We reminisced, and talked about his present activities and the future. He was in philosophic mood, reviewing most interestingly some of his own career and the conclusions he had drawn. This was a personal exchange of views, but I do not think he would mind my relating part of an earlier exchange I had with him when he was still Prime Minister. During a call on him in Parliament House I passed on an invitation from the British Government to join the Heads of Government of the World War II allies for a weekend of events in London commemorating Victory in Europe Day. He could not accept the invitation because of the proximity of the weekend in question to the 1995 Australian National Budget. But he was interested to know what events were to take place. I listed them for him. When I came to the Service at St Paul's Cathedral, that glorious setting for grand occasions and grand music, he leapt to his feet and went to an anteroom, to return with two compact discs. While stressing that the event was nothing to do with him, he suggested that here was the sort of music that ought to be played in St Paul's. One disc was a new recording of Benjamin Britten's *War Requiem*. The other was of music by Elgar. Spot on.

Paul Keating was a tough prime minister to deal with professionally. Also in consonance with the style and qualities of the bilateral relationship, he shied away from no difficulty, and was frank and to the point. He could of course also be subtle and clever in his pursuit of Australian interests. And in international meetings, whether bilateral or multilateral, as indeed in much of his conduct of domestic political business, he was rarely risk-averse. I had first met Paul Keating when he paid an official Head of Government visit to Indonesia. I think this was his first meeting with then President Soeharto. I was interested, and keen to observe each man's handling of the other, so utterly different were they by character, experience and political instinct. But the time was right, in the view of each, for the two countries both to signal and to give effect to an improvement in relations, to their mutual benefit. The resultant diplomatic courtship was conducted in fine style—on both sides. I knew President Soeharto well enough to be unsurprised at his skill. I did not then know Paul Keating, save from press reports. I was much impressed by his careful, well-judged approach to the Indonesian President. Clearly he had done his homework, and was using it very effectively.

John Howard led the Liberal Coalition to a resounding electoral victory over Paul Keating in March 1996. I had known John Howard since our arrival in Australia in 1994 and found him a determined, very able and experienced politician. I also found him a thoroughly decent, accessible and most pleasant man. The epithet 'Honest John' is correct. Hilary and I like the Howards very much. John Howard understands the principles of diplomacy well. He was always open and straight in support of the bilateral relationship and its development. I was conscious that he had been Australia's Minister for Special Trade Negotiations in 1977 at a difficult time consequent on Britain's entry into the then European Common Market. I knew that he had fought the Australian corner very well then; and I thought it possible that he might retain some disappointment with the UK over the eventual outcome. If he did, he showed no sign of it at all. His pursuit of the Australian interest in dealings with Britain—as, I imagine, with other countries—was steadfast and straight. John Howard's public speaking ability, particularly his fluency and comprehensiveness without notes, is well known. In answer to my query when we were once discussing his public speaking, he explained that he has a chronological memory. He uses it most impressively.

John Howard paid an early visit to the new British Government in June 1997. Hilary and I went too, and accompanied John and Janette Howard for much of the visit. I thought it a pity that the visit was quite so dogged by the Australian domestic press, and could have hoped for some more international question and comment. But I was also struck by the extent to which the visit demonstrated that party political opponents could have uninhibited, serious, useful and detailed policy discussions on matters of real social and economic importance to both countries. The rapport John Howard established with British ministers on policy matters recalled for me, in a light-hearted way, an exchange a few years earlier between Paul Keating and then Conservative Deputy Prime Minister Michael Heseltine in Melbourne: they too had found common cause, in this case in discussing tax increases and the electoral factor labelled 'Time for a Change'!

The number of Australian ministers whom I grew to admire and with whom I much enjoyed dealing is large: the list is too long to record. Deputy Prime Minister Tim Fischer was especially good and attentive to diplomats, not just because he was also Minister of Trade and Leader of the National Party. I knew I was going to like him when a few days after our arrival in Australia, a visiting British minister ended their meeting with a personal question: 'How's your farm?' Tim's answer was monosyllabic and highly informative to our English ears. He replied dryly, 'Dry.' I have written about Foreign Minister Alexander Downer earlier. He was always accessible and friendly. Where our interests overlapped, which was often, he was always helpful. Despite the apparent view of a few Australian political cartoonists, I thought he had sublimated his British public school background very effectively!

Tasmania, and Conclusions

I much enjoyed the intellectual challenge of political discourse with Gareth Evans, Alexander Downer's Labor predecessor. Gareth was intellectually testing to work with, on policies of common interest and agreement as well as on the occasional disagreement. We seemed to meet and talk business quite often, and that too, as with Alexander, was a reflection of the co-operation Australia and Britain pursued in multinational diplomacy. Present Opposition Leader Kim Beazley was Treasurer when I first arrived in Australia. Like the others, he was a welcome guest at Westminster House, including in the defence context: he had been a particularly well known and appreciated Minister of Defence, and it was no surprise that he succeeded Paul Keating as Labor leader. Kim Beazley was a contemporary of Tony Blair's at Oxford. The present Australian Minister of Defence Ian McLachlan had earlier studied at 'the other place', Cambridge. Ian played cricket both for Cambridge and for South Australia. His and his wife Janet's Adelaide Test Match cocktail receptions at his house in a leafy Adelaide suburb are also part of cricket history: they are relaxed, stylish and full of cricket greats.

There are, of course, many more able, devoted, hardworking Australian national politicians. RolleroundOz confirmed for me that the Federal nature and geography of Australia mean that national politicians are not as well regarded outside the Federal capital as they should be. Nor are they as well known or as well regarded as their equivalents are in the UK, or even, perhaps, in the USA. Television, radio and national print journalism do not bridge the gap entirely. I suppose this rather sad fact is partly explained by the State structure and allegiances of much of the information media themselves in Australia.

RolleroundOz also illustrated afresh for us the strains between the States and the Commonwealth. One such strain lay behind Premier Richard Court's concern with tax in our discussion in Perth. These strains also explained the need for the High Commission and Consulates-General to lobby not only in Canberra but also in each State capital when, for UK Ltd reasons, we hoped to persuade Australia to change a regulation which affected both Federal and State governments.

Those strains between the States and Canberra also explain some constitutional complications. They explain some of the disregard for Canberra and for things Canberran. They offer some explanation for the view we frequently found during RolleroundOz that the Federal Government (frequently referred to as 'Canberra') neither understands nor cares about problems in the States. One example of that general view is the belief, widely held outside Canberra, that the nation's capital was protected from and did not really know about the last Australian recession. This view of a pampered Canberra may also explain the lack of recognition outside Canberra of the problems stemming from recent public service cuts (I imply no criticism at all of the policy behind those cuts).

I believe the strains also provide part of the explanation for the evident duplication in government—Federal, State and even shire. Some of these problems—and there is a broad range of 'turf' rivalry—are now being addressed. Improvements will no doubt follow. However, the underlying rivalries will not easily fade, partly based as they are on that quintessentially Australian and mostly thoroughly healthy approach to political life: the provision of, and often the insistence upon, checks and balances.

•

As Hilary and I faced my mandatory British Civil Service retirement at 60 (which seems a little ridiculous in these days, although the younger generations seeking promotion and increased responsibility understandably would not agree), and as we Rolled around Oz, we were frequently asked what were the highlights of our time in Australia. This question is a little like 'which was your favourite posting?'. One is comparing apples with cheese and potatoes. But the real difficulty with answering the Australian question is that there are so many highlights that no one should be subjected to the full answer.

A partial answer is: meeting Sir Don Bradman. Conducting business with Paul Keating. The Adelaide Test England won. Conducting business with John Howard. Sailing into Sydney Harbour aboard the Bark *Endeavour*. Being allowed to sit in the House for the opening of the new Northern Territory Parliament Building. Fishing off Arnhem Land. Australia Remembers—and the UK contributions. Most British ministerial visits. The wedding of son Charles and Belinda in the lovely garden at Westminster House. The radical re-design, re-furbishment and re-opening of the British High Commission and the launch of *new*IMAGES. David Malin's stellar photographs taken from the Anglo-Australian Observatory in New South Wales. Many other *new*IMAGES events. Speaking in the Senate Chamber of Old Parliament House. The sale of Hawk as the RAAF's future lead-in fighter-trainer. Visits to Norfolk Island and Lord Howe Island. A visit by Lady Thatcher. The Royal Shakespeare Company's *Dream*. Deep mine visits in the Hunter Valley and Mt Isa. UK naval visits, especially the nine-ship Task Group. Giving an 'Occasional Address' in the Great Hall at the University of Sydney. The Red Arrows visit and displays. Several exhibitions, especially 'Turner' and 'The Queen's Pictures'. Our far north Queensland tour. A similar one in Western Australia. Some joint work on intelligence and assessments. Passage from Sydney to Brisbane in HMS *Monmouth* and '360^0 wing-overs' in the Lynx helicopter. Visiting Maralinga. Each senior official bilateral set of political and economic talks. Sailing in Sydney Harbour and from the Royal Perth Yacht Club. Working with excellent members of two Australian and two British governments, and helping a little to solve just a few problems. The Aussie, as he left Westminster House, saying: 'I want to thank you: I've had a bloody good feed.' And, of course, RolleroundOz.

Thank you, Australia: we had a bloody good time.

INDEX